Map of Nuk Tessli

The Region

che Lk Lookout

ge

dauche Lk

Banana Lk

Whitton Creek

Charlotte Lake

Top Lk

Cowboy Lks

*Halfway Mt.

Fire Rd

Fish Lk

A Mountain Year

Nature Diary of a Wilderness Dweller

A MOUNTAIN YEAR

Nature Diary of a Wilderness Dweller

Chris Czajkowski

Harbour Publishing

DEDICATION

To Alan and Elizabeth Bell.
It is about time you had one!

ACKNOWLEDGEMENTS

An illustrated nature journal is something I have always
wanted to do.
Thank you Harbour Publishing and crew for helping me to
realize my dream.

CONTENTS

PREFACE

In the summer of 1988, I walked into the wilderness and chose a spot on the shore of an unnamed high-altitude lake in the Central Coast Mountains of British Columbia to build two cabins, a business and a life. Twenty years later I still live at Nuk Tessli, from which I operate a small ecotourism business in summer and write, paint and create block prints in winter.

Nuk Tessli (which means "west wind" in the Carrier language) has no road access, and the nearest bush track ends thirty kilometres east. It takes at least fourteen hours to walk to this track in the best of conditions; in winter the journey may last four days. Most visitors and all supplies arrive by single-engine plane, on floats in summer and on skis when the lake is frozen.

I built the first two cabins at Nuk Tessli unaided. Because the site was only three hundred metres below the treeline, it was hard for me to find good building logs. I hunted about for trees that I could use, cut them down with a chainsaw, hauled them by brute force or with a come-along (the ground was too rocky for a wheelbarrow, let alone a horse) and erected them with a combination of skids (sloping poles), ropes and block and tackle.

It took three years to finish both cabins. I lived in a tent until the first was roofed sufficiently to make a shelter and lived in that until the second was built. Then, eight years later, with the help of a young, muscular man to do the heavy logwork, I completed the cabin that is now my home. The first two buildings house clients for the Nuk Tessli Alpine Experience, which caters to hikers and naturalists and other lovers of the wilderness.

I came by this building ability honestly. My father made furniture for a living: his workshop was attached to the house and my toys were woodworking tools. My mum made most of what else we used, and the idea that if you want something you make it seemed most natural to me. And I did not go to Nuk Tessli completely inexperienced in wilderness living. In the early 1980s, I constructed my first off-road log house in a deep coastal valley, on private property surrounded by Tweedsmuir Provincial Park. I had some lifting help and a lot of how-to support from the owners of the property, who had pioneered the place thirty-five years earlier and had lived there in isolation ever since.

Because Nuk Tessli lies on the Interior side of the Coast Mountains, the climate is fairly dry and the stunted high-altitude forest that

surrounds it is mostly pine. There are two species, the strong, universal lodgepole and the weaker, much slower growing whitebark. Subalpine fir is the third common tree species; cottonwood, western red cedar, and both western and mountain hemlock are present, but they rarely push above the winter snow level so exist, where they have been able to take hold, as sprawling bushes. The high-altitude forest, known as "upper-montane" in the botanical world, soon progresses to the subalpine and krummholz levels ("krummholz" means "crooked wood"), after which one arrives at the great sweeps of treeless tundra that are so characteristic of the area.

The region of which my backyard is a small part is known loosely as the Charlotte Alplands. It is situated five hundred kilometres north of Vancouver, on the fringes of the West Chilcotin between the southern tip of Tweedsmuir Provincial Park and Charlotte Lake. It is used by four other tourist operators; I am the only resident. Thanks to Dave Neads and the Anahim Lake Round Table, the area is part of a no-harvest zone where logging and roading are prohibited. In 2004, because of the Lonesome Lake wildfire (which destroyed the homestead where I first built: that cabin is nothing but ashes now), roads were built into the Alplands for firefighting. These roads have been demolished back to the no-log boundary as per the Anahim Lake Round Table Agreement, and the Alplands remains a wilderness area, just as nature made it.

Latin names of all species mentioned in this book are listed in the indexes, pages 164-175.

WINTER

28th December 2004

Cameron Linde could bring his moth-like Piper Supercruiser, fitted with skis for the occasion, right up to the lakeshore below the cabins when he flew me home at noon today. The snow level at Nuk Tessli is much lower than usual, as it is everywhere in the province this year. There are maybe five centimetres on the ice and certainly no more than twenty-five centimetres on land. There was plenty of precipitation during the late fall, but it all came down as rain and ran away. The lack of snow will no doubt have all sorts of ecological repercussions, but there was one advantage: overflow, the water that often sits on ice beneath a heavy snow cover, and which is a bane to pilots, was all but nonexistent. Sometimes at this time of year we have been forced to land three or four hundred metres out into the lake and it has been a nightmare to drag my supplies through the overflow off the ice.

As soon as I, two large dogs and a small amount of freight were unloaded, Cameron took off to fetch a second load. The supplies were waiting in my Suburban, which was sitting on the ice at Nimpo Lake, forty kilometres north, and the return trip would take him a little over an hour. By the time he came back, I had broken trail to the cabin, lit the two stoves and thawed a big metal bowl of snow so that there was enough bark-flecked water to make Cameron a cup of tea. Melting snow for water is a nuisance, particularly when the covering is so scanty. My usual source is lake water, but the job of cutting a hole in the ice had to be put off, as all my energies during what was left of the daylight were concentrated on securing the freight.

29th December 2004

It has warmed to minus 5°C and it is mild and grey and windless.

I brought the chainsaw in last night so that it would thaw out, and cut the waterhole this morning. Waterholes always shrink inward during cold spells so I make them about a metre across. The ice was surprisingly thick considering the mildness of the fall, and the bar sank in for about thirty centimetres before it broke through. Instantly, water fountained up the whirling chain. Beads of water froze like pearls on my upper clothes and my pant legs became stiff with ice.

The bottom half of the ice was clear as glass and hard as iron and the rest was weaker, opaque snow-ice. Sometimes it is half that depth at this time of year; snow is a good insulator and without it, the ice has had a better chance to form. I made the hole five-sided, and after I had cut pie-shaped wedges and levered them out with the peavey and axe, a stark, black pentangle sat like a belligerent eye on the soft mantle of white. The water surface was exactly level with the top of the ice and as motionless as a mirror. My face and the overcast sky were reflected darkly in it.

31st December 2004

Much colder: minus 22°C and a mist snow. The flakes are minute, yet the precipitation is more solid than freezing fog and does not adhere to surfaces but stays dry and loose. It never accumulates much, but it hazes the world so that not only the big mountains at the head of the lake but also the smaller ones across from my cabin are hidden, and the islands ringing the point have a misty blue cast. There is very little wind and it is coming from the east; when the overhead veil thins, I can dimly see higher clouds barrelling in from the west. A couple of years ago I built a porch around the cabin door; sometimes, when it is really cold and this wind is blowing, a rim of hoar collects along the bottom of the door and the nailheads facing the room acquire a fur of frost.

It is these conditions that endow the coast with its terrible southeast storms. Warm air rises from the ocean and causes cold air from the Interior to rush in to replace it. Because the gaps through the mountains are few, the cold air is funnelled and it gathers tremendous speed as it drops down to the sea.

The lack of sun means I will have to forgo the use of the electric light if I want my computer to have any power. It and the satellite internet are operated by a photovoltaic system that is more than adequate when the sun shines, even at this time of year. Right now, two candles in a bowl backed by a pair of hinged mirror tiles propped in a V shape illuminate my activities at night.

A red squirrel clatters around the eaves, much to the excitement of the dogs. It is the first living

Red squirrel

creature I have seen. The two mice that have been caught in the traps since I got home were already dead.

1st January 2005

The heavens were hidden but the night was bright with a silvery soup of moonlight refracted off snowflakes fine as stardust. Dawn brought minus 22°C temperatures and a fog of snowdust and ice crystals. The wind chill was quite severe, catching my lungs and freezing the mucus in my nose. I had to take my glasses off as they fogged up with my breath, then froze; I could see blurry spangles of frost on my eyelashes.

There is a trail I call "The Block." It follows a creek up as far as Otter Lake—named after the otter tracks I see there most winters—then back through a series of meadows, arriving at the lakeshore about half a kilometre from home. I usually ski back on the ice, but if the wind is too bad, I break trail home through the forest. It takes about forty minutes to walk The Block in summer if you don't stop to look at anything, but winter times vary and the first trudge of the season is always slow. This year's covering of snow was too thin to smooth the ground between the boulders and fallen trees so made for some tight ski wriggling. The top of the snow was soft and formless, but halfway down was a crust, formed no doubt during the pre-Christmas rains, which sometimes held the skis up and sometimes didn't. I have no skill on the snow and use the barnboard-wide skis with skins more like snowshoes, but the trail gets better through the winter, and when the snow gets deeper and settles more, I will be able to go farther afield.

To reach Otter Creek, I must cross Cabin Meadow ("meadow" is a euphemism for "bog" in this part of the world). All frozen now, of course, but much more open, and there I saw squirrel and ptarmigan tracks, and pawprints of what I am pretty sure was a wolf. They were somewhat drifted in, but no other animal could have made marks that size. It wouldn't have been the dogs: they drag their feet and make a continuous trough in the snow, whereas, unless it is very deep, each wolf paw plops in and makes a distinct and separate hole. Ptarmigan make a continuous track, too, a convoluted waddle winding around exposed willow twigs like an Andy Goldsworthy sand drawing. They must be able to distinguish willow buds while on the wing because they never land near the similar-sized mountain azalea, which I must get quite close to in order to differentiate.

There was no sign of life in the forest. Otter Creek was higher than normal because of the rains and also much more open. Where it looped through a tiny meadow, the ice was so thin that one of my dogs, Raffi, who is spending his first winter in the bush, leapt straight onto it and immediately crashed into the water. My other dog, Bucky, who has been with me for a couple of years, looked on with equanimity. Dogs do not have an instinctive knowledge of ice, as many people think; they have to learn about it like everyone else. Raffi pulled himself out immediately and seemed none the worse for his ducking, but he was a great deal more cautious after that.

Later in the day, the mist snow slowly began to thin. The sun grew strong enough to cast pale shadows, and Louise O'Murphy, the mountain across the lake from the cabin, appeared ethereal as a ghost above grey billows of fog. Toward the head of the lake the sun was low and too bright to look at as it set into an orange haze of ice crystals. The shapes of the western mountains, Monarch and Migma, which are among the main bulwarks of the Coast Range, emerged as chalky blue cutouts. In front of them, growing brighter by the moment, a shard of rainbow trailed onto the lake. It was a sundog, caused by the sun reflecting on the airborne ice. At this time of year the sun sets behind a group of rocks and trees, so I had to step onto the lake to see the other sundog, a multicoloured slash by now as brilliant as stained glass. Parhelions (if you want to use the technical term) occur when the ice crystals are long and six-sided, rather like very small pencils, and the air is calm enough for them to be suspended vertically. Flat, six-sided ice crystals cause a sun pillar, and there was one of those, too. Long after the sun and its dogs had disappeared, this column of light poked like a soft orange searchlight into the sky.

2nd January 2005

Minus 25°C first thing and clear, glorious sunshine. A Delftware blue-and-white day. The sun rose in a cloudless sky to paint the western mountains blood red, neon orange, salmon, yellow, then white. Now it is evening; the glorious sun has gone but soft mauve and rosy bands of colour lie behind the white hummocks of Louise O'Murphy, indicating another fine day tomorrow. I can allow myself the luxury of the electric light tonight. I don't mind how cold it gets as long as I have sun; the downside is that I have to chop more ice from the waterhole—five centimetres this morning.

Mid-morning, a *whop* of wings and a Clark's nutcracker arrived at my feeder, followed shortly by a second. I had flown in some lumps of cow fat begged from a butcher who lives not far from Nimpo, and tied it tightly to a pole fixed near a window, between the eaves and the wall. The fat freezes hard and the birds pound away at it in fine style. The two

Clark's nutcrackers

nutcrackers were getting on with each other so I assumed they were a pair—there is not much room on the feeding pole and unrelated birds will scrap. These two are whacking off finger-joint-sized pieces and gulping them whole. Nutcrackers apparently have throat pouches in which to carry conifer seeds, but I can see no swelling there so assume they are swallowing the fat chunks straight down. They seem to be able to ingest huge quantities.

I've often wondered how they recognize it, as white fat alone would be an anomaly in nature. A carcass is another matter: red blood is like a flag on the snow. But suet blends in. Most birds are not supposed to have a sense of smell, but their brains have different components than ours. Memory centres like those in a human are absent in birds, so it was once thought that they were stupid—hence the term "bird brain." But it has since been discovered that they remember with an organ we don't possess. Brains are complicated things. The mechanism of migration, for instance, has not been categorically determined despite much study. Perhaps their scent sensor has not been isolated yet.

In the afternoon it warmed to a balmy minus 10°C and I ski-plodded up the north shore of the lake and then back down the middle. In one spot a few snowshoe hare tracks headed way across the lake, but there were no other marks. I ran into a really bad bit of overflow where the ice had cracked. I saw a slightly greyish sunken area, but because the snow cover was thin I assumed it had frozen. I sloshed right into water—even my ski boots were wet. Exposed to the air, the sludge instantly froze and the skis became ten-ton weights. I chipped and scraped off what I could, but it was heavy work coming home.

4th January 2005

Minus 25°C to minus 5°C. The third gorgeous day in a row. Eight centimetres of ice this morning—the waterhole has already shrunk alarmingly.

I broke trail down Cranberry Meadows, a series of bogs that run more or less parallel to the lake about half a kilometre south. They were named (by me) for the bog cranberries that grow there.

There are several species of plants called "cranberry" in North America. Two grow in my backyard. Highbush cranberries cluster around Otter Creek and in a few other damp places, but they are at the upper limit of their range. The bog cranberry, however, is right at home. Some summers its tiny reflexed pink blossoms are thick among the sphagnum mosses and short, waterlogged sedges. I occasionally find green berries on the hair-thin creeping stalks later in the year, but they are always covered with snow before they ripen. Apparently they can mature beneath the snow and are no doubt consumed by small creatures, as there is no sign of them in the spring.

Partway through the meadows I use a remnant of a neglected trap trail that goes through a thick patch of subalpine fir. The bark on two of the trees is strongly ridged, indicating age. Both have holes chopped in them, creating small platforms; this is where meat would have been fixed with a nail. The leghold traps that were still legal when the trapline was being operated hung from sloping poles attached immediately below the platforms. The traps would have been set for American marten. This

Trap tree

trapline comes all the way from Charlotte Lake. The trapping family I knew when I first came here travelled this far back because they liked living in the bush; in any case, fur prices were better then. But that family has sold out and dispersed. I believe someone is active at the Charlotte Lake end, where there is easy snow-machine access, but I do not know who, as many trappers fear animal-rights activists and keep that information secret.

6th January 2005

Warm enough in the sun yesterday so that the thin layer of snow slid off the roof. There was some wind last night but the sky was clear and the late moon rose unhindered. The thermometer registered minus 15°C but there was a far greater bite to the wind than one would expect from that temperature. On my early trek to the outhouse I had to keep changing the hand that held the flashlight and thrusting the other into my down coat pocket to warm up.

By dawn, both sun and mountains were swallowed by more mist snow. An hour later, a furious northeast wind started, blowing the thin accumulation off the roof like smoke. It is the west wind, *nuk tessli*, that is the most powerful here; east winds rarely have much push, but some of today's gusts must have reached gale force. Everything in the porch was soon covered with a fine white powder, blown in through the gaps around the dog door.

A third Clark's nutcracker has appeared. It grabs fat when the others let it. The dominant two went through what must have been a pair-bonding ritual several times during the day. They touched beaks and made a rapid clicking noise rather like an old spring alarm clock being wound up.

11th January 2005

During the night, the wind gradually died and a few stars came out. By daylight it was minus 30°C.

Right in front of the outhouse is a rotten stump, and at its base this morning was a perfect wingprint in the snow. It was too small for a nutcracker, and a little while later, a female hairy woodpecker came to the feeder.

She pounds the fat when the nutcrackers fly away. She is not particularly frightened of them, just happy to defer to their greater size. She often examines the cabin wall beside the feeding pole when the nutcrackers are busy.

When I decided to put the pole in that particular spot, I did not

Hairy woodpeckers

realize that every peck the birds made would be audible inside the cabin. Each creature has its own feeding rhythm so I hardly need look out the window to know what is there. The woodpeckers (the downy woodpecker comes sometimes) have a neat little trick I would never have noticed were it not for the soundbox effect of my four walls. After a few whacks, there is a short, rapid vibrating; the individual sounds are so close together they are barely distinguishable. I have observed that after the bird has partially separated a bit of fat, it is able to grasp it in its beak and thrash its head back and forth in a blur, in an attempt to loosen it further. It must be a very useful technique to make bugs relinquish their hold on tight crevices. It occurs so quickly I would never have noticed it if I had not been able to hear it.

12th January 2005

Minus 22°C at sunup, but it never went above minus 12°C. Calm at first so I decided to ski up the lake, but two-thirds of the way along, a sudden bitter wind drove me back. The skis flopped onto wind crust and the poles squealed or moaned depending on the snow depth. The surface of the lake is very hummocky; the snow is carved into miniature dunes and frozen waves. There are a number of big cracks, and I watched very carefully for overflow. In one instance the crack had split vertically, which is most unusual. One side was at least a centimetre higher than the other.

15th January 2005

The thermometer read minus 25°C, but it felt much warmer because the wind has lost its bite. The radio tells me all sorts of snow is forecast for the Lower Mainland; the computer tells me that Bella Coola on the other side of the big mountains is supposed to have rain. We need snow desperately; several years' drought has cut back the pack drastically. I used to consider a metre depth around the cabins to be a low snow year (occasionally it has been two metres deep), but even that low mark has not been reached for some time and at the moment it barely reaches my knees.

16th January 2005

Still, dull and minus 8°C when I first awoke. It was a real surprise to see three centimetres of fresh snow, as I usually wake on and off during the night and had not been aware of it falling.

I caught a different mouse in the attic last night. It was a deermouse, but the subspecies that lives at higher altitudes, with an extraordinarily long tail.

I found a dead one in the alpine once but otherwise never see them. It is the first creature to succumb to my trapline for a couple of weeks—I trapped three animals on the first three nights I was home, and all four are different species. The others were a "normal"

Long-tailed deermouse

deermouse, a fat, dark lemming, probably the northern bog lemming, and the smaller red-backed vole.

Two mountain chickadees competed with the Clark's nutcracker and female hairy woodpecker at the feeder today. And when I skied The Block, I saw a spruce grouse and also the snowboard tracks that river otters make at (where else?) Otter Lake. The temperature climbed to plus 1°C this afternoon and the roof dripped. Exposed rocks, which are at present much colder than the air, have acquired a thick fur of hoar-frost.

17th January 2005

Rain! Actually, it was hard to tell whether it was rain or snow. It was white but plummeted straight down with the speed and weight of liquid water, and it dripped off the trees as soon as it landed. It was extraordinarily dark all day. The showers/flurries (slurries?) came and went at first, but later the precipitation was continuous.

I took advantage of the warmth to wash some heavier clothes—wool longjohns, some pants and a sweater. They could do the majority of their dripping outside. The snow crashed off Cabin Two's roof and made a mess of my trail to the outhouse. If left there, it would solidify into an unwieldy lump; if it froze it would be a disaster. So I shovelled it out of the way in heavy, wet dollops. The trunks of the trees are rain-black, the foliage dark and heavy. Under the dripping branches are yellow stains.

Three mountain chickadees came to the fat today. I put up a new

Mountain
chickadees

piece and chopped up the ragged remnants of the old one into the dogs' dishes.

18th January 2005

Plus 4°C and dripping. The water splats and plops into a line of pockmarks it has made in the waterlogged slush under the eaves.

I don't know what it is doing in the Lower Mainland; radio reception comes in and out with the weather and I couldn't get a squeak out of the radio this morning.

19th January 2005

Some pretty heavy rain yesterday. It eased toward evening, but when I woke at night I could hear more plopping and dripping, and also the hiss of rain on the bare metal roof. It has to come down quite heavily for that to be audible. Rain falls in January on occasion, but it usually doesn't last longer than a day or two. The trails to the outhouse and waterhole are rotted through and I need snowshoes to walk on them. When the cloud level lifted a bit, I could see bare trees right up to the alpine so it must be raining at quite a high altitude.

A red-breasted nuthatch arrived at the feeder today. Its breast was quite pale so it must have been a female. One often hangs about with a small group of mountain chickadees in the winter, and the nuthatch always bosses the chickadees. Do they have an affinity with each other because both species have white eyebrows?

And now it is dark again, but there is a paleness to it. A waning moon is fuzzily visible—just over half full. Vapour is rushing silently in front of it with the speed of an express train. It is dead calm down here, not a hint of air movement. The sky wind is coming from the southwest, shooting straight up here from Hawaii.

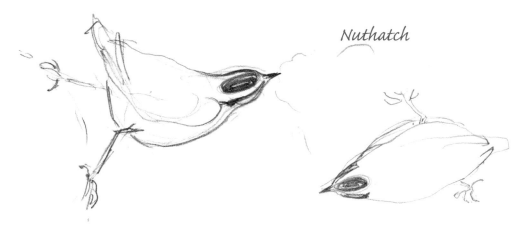

Nuthatch

20th January 2005

I woke to clearer weather and an eerily brilliant glow of filtered moonlight on the snow. It occurred to me that the temperature might be dropping; sure enough, the porch thermometer read plus 1°C. If it got colder, any sloppy snow on the solar panels would freeze. I have been getting very low on power these last few dark days and did not want to waste a scrap of daylight waiting for ice to thaw. I took the flashlight and slithered down to the lakeshore, where the frame holding the panels looks over the ice. Sure enough, a sludge was already hardening onto the panels. I scraped it off, but after I had gone back to bed and the night grew darker, indicating that the moon had set, I heard the drum of rain again, and then the steady splat of water in the pockmarks under the eaves. By daylight there was a new sound. The slush below the eaves had melted away and the drips plopped onto bare wood.

Poor conditions or not, I had to get out of the house, and I headed for The Block. I figured the snow would be too wet to stick to the skis and I was right, but oh, what a struggle! Every two or three steps I crashed into a hole, skis and all. The baskets on the poles had no resistance and kept dropping into space, then snagging on branches when I wanted to pull them out. On my way back across the lake, the overflow was terrible and the skis slopped through it.

22nd January 2005

Plus 1°C and absolutely pouring! This is getting ridiculous.

A second nuthatch has arrived at the fat. This one has a redder breast so presumably is a male. I did a few sketches of them. They are great acrobats, posing beautifully at impossible angles.

Most winters, only one nuthatch is present and the chickadees get time at the fat. But the two of them are ganging up on the smaller birds and the poor little chickadees can hardly get a peck in.

24th January 2005

Fog-filtered moonlight. The steady drip of rain. Then the wind started and pulled the vapour into flying rags. The moon was close to setting so the cabin was in shadow, but Louise O'Murphy broke through the vapour and was seemingly lit by an internal phosphorescence. The surface of the lake is now grey, and puddles of water are lying on it. They ruffle in the gusts of wind, but behind Kojo's Island is a calm pool and the ghost ship of the mountain was reflected in it.

I am not getting enough exercise in these difficult travel conditions and it is making me very frustrated, so I looked forward to walking on the bare ice of the lake. The grey surface, however, was not ice at all, but ankle-deep sludge. My boots got soaked just trudging to the waterhole.

In order to be outside in the watery sun for a while, I wrapped up well and took a chair onto the half-bare deck. I was close to the fat pole, and the birds were very active. Two nutcrackers, two nuthatches, two mountain chickadees and the one female hairy woodpecker. I could recognize the birds by the sound of their wings alone, from the *whop whop* of the nutcrackers to the *frrrrp* of the chickadees. The chickadees might have been at the bottom of the birds' totem pole, but they were the least frightened of me so they got a longer than usual feed. They whizzed close to my head several times, and one actually perched on my wool hat—I could feel his little claws digging into my scalp.

Mountain chickadee

26th January 2005

Now there is a noise I should not be able to hear until spring—the roar of the river where it tips out of the lake directly across from the cabin. At first light I shuffled around there, keeping to the thin white edge of the ice when I could, but sometimes having to cross onto the grey stuff. The sludge now holds the skis up in places; the weakest areas are in the transition zone between white and grey. The river is angry, dark and green where it tumbles into the rapids.

Three gray jays arrived at the fat. Most years I don't often see them by the cabin, although I run into them in the bush once in a while. At the feeder they defer to the larger nutcrackers.

Gray jay

29th January 2005

Cooler at last and a bit of sunshine. There were a few flurries at first and I hoped they were wet enough to stick to the ice and provide some traction, but they were driven by a wild southwest wind that scoured the ice clean and polished it more than ever. Cloud layers showed that higher up the winds were different—the middle layer came from the west, and a much higher upper layer was travelling from the northwest. This could be a good sign: if the wind moves clockwise it usually means it is going to get cooler and clearer. However, if the wind moves counter-clockwise, the weather most often deteriorates. Sometimes the improvement is very brief and the wind flips right back again before we get any benefit from it. Heavy clouds still hang over the mountains in the west.

31st January 2005

Some extremely violent gusts last night. The constant roar and boom gets to me after a while, so I went to sleep wearing ear protectors. They don't cut the noise out entirely but they do help.

I awoke to less wind and a mist of refracted moonlight. I could barely see the far shore of the lake so knew that snow must be falling. Daylight revealed it plastered on one side of the trees and piled against the bottom of the windows like fake snow on a Christmas card. It's hard to judge the depth when it blows about so much, but it is more sheltered near the outhouse and, judging by my tracks there, maybe four centimetres fell. The thermometer read plus 4°C by the afternoon, and most of it disappeared.

3rd February 2005

It looks like it is going to be a six-day storm. We usually get two or three of them every winter. It was squally all day on the first, and snowed and blew a terrible gale all day yesterday. The whole building was plastered with snow, and patches of the ground most exposed to the wind have been blown bare. There was quite an accumulation this time—maybe twenty centimetres. This, I thought, was a bit more promising.

But this morning I woke to find everything thawing furiously. Wind slightly less intense but still a good gale. Will there be any end to this horrible weather?

4th February 2005

The wind. Finally. Stopped.

To be surrounded by such utter silence after days of bombardment is like falling into a hole. And at last it is a little cooler. At sundown yesterday there was some clearing with a few pink clouds, and this morning the temperature was minus 4°C.

I skied The Block early while everything was still frozen. The tracks were less icy because of the new snow, and the lake was perfect! A skiff of white to give traction but otherwise slick and fast. It is so rare to get real skiing conditions here (at least, that is what I tell myself: actually, it is I who can't ski). In windier spots the lake has been swept clear and long streaks of grey glare ice are showing, but they are frozen hard and the snow patches are big enough to let me get around the ice.

I have been trying to arrange a flight out within the next ten days or so. I have to go to Vancouver to do a wilderness first aid course. Cameron is too busy with his family-run sawmill, but a local logger, Duke, has put skis on his plane and he will fly me out when he has time. He may not be able to give a lot of notice, so I have started packing up ready to leave. I don't expect to be away for more than a couple of weeks, but I have to batten the place down against warm temperatures and even bears, as well as winter conditions, in case something happens and I don't get back. It takes several days to make the place properly secure. I don't need to be in Vancouver until the 21st, but will have to accept my ride when weather and Duke's schedule allow it.

5th February 2005

Minus 13°C this morning! Brilliant stars, but daylight brought a haze of cloud in from the west. At first, parts of Monarch and Migma were visible, although veiled in curtains of snow, but now they have disappeared again.

Dipper

Lake travel was so easy I went past the head of my lake and along the short stretch of river to the next one, and then back home through Cranberry Meadows to check for American dippers. They are present in either one spot or the other most winters because even during the coldest spells, stretches of open water remain there.

I have been keeping bird records for what is now called the Biodiversity Centre for Wildlife Studies, an organization initiated by British Columbia's bird guru, Wayne Campbell. When I first presented my winter observations to him he expressed surprise that American dippers wintered at such a high altitude. The birds take advantage of a very specialized niche in nature. They are distant relatives of thrushes (and about the same size) but have acquired very long toes and the ability to walk under water in swiftly flowing streams. They live off aquatic insects, notably blackfly larvae that cling to underwater rocks, and use their long toes to grasp the stones as they forage along the bottom. Without webbed feet they cannot swim efficiently, and were it not for the toes' grasp, they would bob to the surface like corks. Their feathers are so dense and finely barbed that they are waterproof and they also insulate the bird against the subzero cold; were the water not tumbling through rapids, it would certainly freeze. Even during the warmest days of rain this year, my waterhole always made a bit of ice.

Dipper

On this day I neither saw nor heard any dippers. There were plenty of open spots because of the much greater than normal volume roaring down the rapids, but I wondered if the birds would be able to feed in such fierce conditions. The water was a dark, greenish black, the foam a dirty grey. The ice accumulating on the rocks and fallen trees looked dirty, too. Frozen spray had formed wondrous icicles that hung from bulging rocks and trees that have fallen into the water. The icicles are wider at the bottom than the top, culminating in bulbous clubs with a series of smaller, frilly icicle teeth along the bottom.

8th February 2005

It's like spring out there! It was minus 14°C this morning but clear and sunny all day, and it warmed to just below freezing during the afternoon. On the same date last year it was minus 32°C, and the year before it was minus 37°C! It's the first time I have seen the sunrise and sunset points for a while. The rising sun now has to climb over the long shoulder of Louise O'Murphy, so it takes quite a while to appear. Its emergence point seems to move very slowly. But there is a marked difference where the sun sets. When I flew in here, a week after the shortest day, the sun would bury itself among the trees behind the rock pile near the southwest corner of the cabin. Now it not only breaks clear of these trees, it also rides right over the top of Mount Monarch, giving me a good half-hour of extra sunshine.

I skied up the north shore of the lake and ran into several ptarmigan beds where the snow had drifted a little deeper in the lee of small protuberances along the shore. These birds prefer to overnight right

Willow ptarmigan

in the middle of the lake, but there is not enough snow for them to do that this year. I love to find their beds—from a distance they are just a slash in the pristine white, but close up you can see the skid marks of the feet and braking tail and wings; the deeper hole, sometimes littered with kibble-like droppings, in which they spend the night; and then the walking prints dissolving into two or three perfect sets of wingmarks on the snow as they take off again. In the alpine, in the summer, I have encountered three species of ptarmigan, the rock and willow being the most common, the white-tailed rarer, but the only one to winter around the cabins is the willow ptarmigan. The black eyes and beak, and black edge to the tail are the only things visible when they are standing in the snow. I never see them until they move.

Other tracks showed that a few squirrels and snowshoe hares had passed this way, and also a member of the dog family, most likely a red fox.

The radio says the weather is supposed to deteriorate in a couple of days. I hope Duke manages to pick me up before then.

9th February 2005

Got an email about 10:00 a.m. saying that Duke may be in this afternoon, so I packed everything except the computer. But he did not come. At 6:00 p.m. another email told me he will try to get in tomorrow. I hope it is early—it is getting windy again and clouds are building up in the west. Patches between them allowed a dusky orange light through to Louise O'Murphy at sundown, and above it were piled lenticular clouds, which Richard Proenneke in *One Man's Wilderness* very aptly called windbags. They do not stream along like other clouds but pile up in the lee of a mountain, sometimes looking like a tottering stack of flapjacks. They are always a sign of strong winds.

10th February 2005

Sunny but wild and windy, and a considerable amount of blowing snow on the surface of the lake. Duke got in, but he could barely turn his plane around in order to enter the channel between the islands. "I had no idea it was as bad as this up here," he said cheerfully. A lot of people don't realize how much stronger the winds can be at Nuk Tessli. "It keeps me on my toes," Duke added, grinning. Not what someone who is uncomfortable with flying wants to hear. But with the wind behind us, we had a really fast trip to Nimpo.

SPRING

2nd March 2005

Everything outside went according to schedule, but what with doing the first aid course, giving two slide shows, driving to Vancouver and back, buying a few hard-to-get supplies, answering snail mail and doing all the phone business I possibly could, then waiting until Duke was available, it is almost three weeks since I last set foot on the place. Despite an unprecedented spell of endless sunshine the whole time I was away, it was dull and windy when Duke flew me home yesterday. Conditions were not too bad until we crossed Charlotte Lake and entered the mountains proper, but then the flight got bumpier and bumpier until we popped over the final ridge and glided onto the lake. Fortunately there was not much air movement on the ground. Nimpo Lake had no snow on the ice at all; the surface was a solid grey glare as slick as glass. Here the lake had a thin, sugary covering so there was enough traction to haul the toboggan-loads of freight off the ice without difficulty.

I was greeted by the male red-breasted nuthatch, but there was no trace of fat on the feeding pole. I will put some up there today. When I arrived, there was a deermouse in a trap in the attic, and last night I caught a red-backed vole. I did some sketches of it but it is hard to make the critter seem alive when it is not.

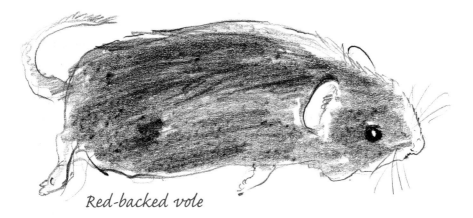

Red-backed vole

4th March 2005

Dull and windy. Barely freezing again last night. What a bummer to have wasted all that gorgeous weather down in Vancouver.

I put the skis on and trudged around The Block. It was thawing again, the thin surface snow slushy, with the texture of coarse salt. The only sign of life was wolf tracks at Otter Lake, but they must have been old as neither dog gave them so much as a sniff.

steller's jay

6th March 2005

A wild night and a squally day yesterday, driving wet snow onto all the windward surfaces. But today the wind had lessened and a hazy sun showed through. It was very warm and the birds loved it.

There were two Clark's nutcrackers, two nuthatches, two gray jays, the female hairy woodpecker and a male hairy, his red nape patch brilliant. And, most unusual for here, a Steller's jay.

There was also a red squirrel at the fat today, which explained why the dogs have been tearing around the cabin and staring ecstatically at the eaves, but it doesn't explain their similar behaviour at least three times last night. Red squirrels are daytime creatures. One year the fat attracted a marten, but it snarled most fearsomely whenever the dogs came around and I heard no noise this time.

7th March 2005

Rain again last night! This winter is unbelievable. I don't think I have ever recorded rain in March before. I well remember one trip I made in here on snowshoes at this time of year, not long after I first came to Nuk Tessli, when the temperature dropped to 40 below.

I brought meat in with me; it is frozen solid and I can usually keep it for a while, but because of this terrible weather I will have to can it right away. Butchering is a job I hate because I am no good at it. But even while I struggle and curse to separate the joints and clean away the fat and gristle, I cannot help but marvel how intricately everything is put together. It is the transition from one kind of tissue to the other, such as tendon to muscle, that fascinates me most. Having just learned about all sorts of body parts in the first aid course, I found the job even more interesting! I also thought about the master artists such as Leonardo da Vinci delicately separating his illegally disinterred corpses in the dead of night in order to learn how the human body worked. After hacking away for all these years, I still can't separate joints cleanly.

8th March 2005

I know who my secret night visitor is! I heard a delicate gnawing, crept out of bed to reach for the flashlight, fumbled for my glasses and then trained the light on the fat pole and switched it on. I needn't have been cautious, for the little animal totally ignored me and kept on feeding. It was a northern flying squirrel. I have seen these only once before at Nuk Tessli, about a dozen years ago, when a group of three or four hung about for a few days in the winter.

About the same size as the red squirrel, the flying squirrel is otherwise a very different animal. It has large, protruding night-vision eyes; round, hairless, papery ears; a tail from which the hairs spread sideways only, and much smaller toes than the day squirrel. And of course the great flap of skin used for gliding. It is fascinating how that enormous expanse folds up so efficiently when the animal is not airborne.

The flying squirrel can apparently glide for fifty metres and change direction in mid-air. The little *pok* as it lands on a tree is like no other sound. The undeveloped digits are a great disadvantage for the animal on the ground, making it easy prey for terrestrial predators. For most people, the only indication that these creatures are around is a feather-flat tail lying in front of their contented cat.

Shortly after the squirrel left, it started to rain. It rained for the rest of the night and all the following day.

10th March 2005

At last! A gorgeous spring day. So warm I sat on my newly shovelled deck without a coat on. For some reason the birds were largely absent—they are usually more active in better weather, but perhaps it was so good they were finding treats among the trees. It grew windy later, and

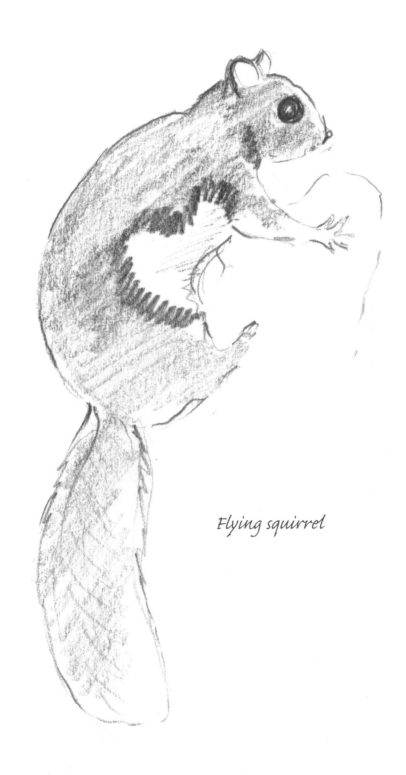

Flying squirrel

the Steller's jay came for a brief visit. It has surprisingly long and unruly feathers and they were much tossed by the wind, giving the bird a very ragged look. The female hairy was at the feeder, too.

A couple of flies buzzed against the cabin wall in the warmth, and inside, a spider let itself down on a rope of silk. How do spiders survive the winter? What do they feed on before the insects become active? It is really miraculous how swiftly spiders can make silk. But what I find most amazing of all is how they reabsorb it so quickly when they climb back up their thread. Where does all that fibre go in such a tiny body? And how is it stored? As coils of silk, or is it immediately dissolved back into its components? One visitor I mentioned this to said they have a little rewind spring, as in a retractable tape measure.

There was a touch of frost first thing today, and with difficulty I slithered around The Block. Everything was extremely icy. The lake is mostly grey again after yesterday's hot sun and it was treacherous. A thin skin of ice lay over about five centimetres of grey sludge, so I picked my awkward way back along the intermittent band of sloping white beside the shore. Where it was absent, I made cautious slides across the ice and water. I knew there was good ice underneath, but it is disconcerting to know that you may crash through the surface at any moment.

There was no sign of life away from the cabin, largely because this icy snow surface doesn't show marks—in other years I have seen tracks of mouse, weasel, mink, marten, hare, ptarmigan and possibly wolf or fox. I did see one sign of spring, though. In three places, the tiny silvery buttons of pussy willow buds were just starting to show. A number of species of willow grow in this area, and they all flower at different times. Some are easy enough to identify but this particular species has no obvious features and remains a mystery to me.

11th March 2005

The satellite weather forecast was for mixed cloud and frost, but it rained quite heavily last night. It cleared toward afternoon and became balmy and springlike again. Shortly after sundown, while it was still light enough to read, I heard two great horned owls, presumably a pair because their calls were pitched about an octave apart. *Keep awake— with me!* I do not hear owls all that often here, have seen them twice and have never found pellets. You would think they would be more common, as there are plenty of small rodents. Mice often make tracks far out onto the lake and cross from side to side, a distance of at least a kilometre. They would surely be easy pickings for an owl.

12th March 2005

Cloudless, windless, brilliant sun! What a day!

It cleared last night and I kept my fingers crossed for a frost. There were six whole degrees of it in the morning and I grabbed a lunch and the skis and set off before the sun had reached the cabin. Destination— the North Ridge. I generally manage to get at least partway up it by the end of January. But what with the weather and being away for three weeks, my first excursion in this direction is much later this year.

There were few trails in this territory when I first came here, and the ones that existed were winter trails that the trapper used and in very poor shape for hiking. But I have brushed out several routes to provide easier access to the alpine. At lower elevations, in summer, the one to the North Ridge is now obvious because of the wear on the ground. But to define it before traffic grew heavy, I cut blazes on the trees and built rock cairns for the areas where trees were spaced too far apart. The blazes give me a good indication of snow depth. During my first winters at Nuk Tessli, the blazes would often be buried by snow, but this year they are all exposed. A good metre of trunk is showing below them near the cabins, but at Otter Lake the snow is at least thirty centimetres deeper. At subalpine levels the blazes were less than knee high, so there is some kind of a pack higher up.

Across Otter Lake, the route climbs gradually at first but then there is a steep bit that cannot be avoided. It is never easy because of the rocks and fallen trees, especially when the snow is so shallow, but I know no way around it. The snow was well glazed and I sank not at all; when I had to traverse a steep slope, which was frequently, the steel edges of the skis could not dig in and I often skidded sideways. I gambled that there would be some surface melting to improve traction before I came down.

Apart from the *yank yank* of a nuthatch near Otter Lake and a couple of mountain chickadees a little higher, there was not a flicker of movement or peep of any living thing. The heavy rains had created an unusual landscape for this time of year. All kinds of creeks gurgled beneath the snow in places where I had no idea water ever ran, and I was astounded to see quantities of bare ground in a couple of subalpine meadows where running surface water had melted the snow from below. The country looked more like May than March.

Through the krummholz level I encountered a skiff of fresh snow over the rain-glazed surface. In summer I usually go east to avoid a huge rockslide, but now I could plod straight up it; only a few boulders poked above the blanket of white. Hoary marmots and pikas live here, and I thought of them as I skied over their homes, the marmots drugged by hibernation and the pikas running their busy lives through their rocky tunnels, feasting on the hay they had so assiduously dried and gathered during the summer. Below me was the dark forest slashed by the pale ice of my lake, and beyond it more forest backed by an immense panorama of peaks, many of them unnamed, the highest of which was over four thousand metres. This was Mount Waddington; its summit would be at least a hundred kilometres distant but it was perfectly clear in the azure sky.

Then onto the wide plateau that is home to calendar-picture flower meadows in July and August. Several small peaks form the ridge behind it and two of these, situated side by side, have seductively curved profiles with small bumps on top. A client took one look at them and said: "Ah, the Mammaries!" They are aptly named.

Once away from the edge of the rockslide, I could not see my valley, and I was enveloped in a wind-smoothed world of trackless white marked only by the subtle patterns carved by the wind. My ski tracks pencilled a thin, angular line behind me. Bucky's smaller pawprints stayed within my marks—he is ever the lazy one—but Raffi had zigzagged back and forth continuously, his trail looping and snaking like a tangled skein of wool. Eat your heart out, Andy Goldsworthy.

Time to turn around. The thin covering of fresh snow was beginning to stick a little, but if I kept moving it did not clog the skis too badly. I am a terrible skier so allowed myself only gentle glides and did a lot of zigzagging. The dogs were unused to me going faster than walking pace and, because they sank farther, were hard pressed to keep up. It was quite amusing to see their puzzled and slightly desperate faces as they struggled along behind me. Below the krummholz layer, the snow surface had disintegrated to the granular slush I had hoped for, so the plod downward was not too difficult. A better skier would have covered the distance in a fraction of the time. But for me, experiencing the wilderness has nothing to do with the speed at which I can cover it or the heights I can gain, but with just being there.

14th March 2005

The woodpeckers are frequent visitors to the feeder; they are always noisy birds with their shrill whistles, and now they have started to drum. The nutcrackers visit the fat less frequently now. One March, I found a pair crooning (if one can apply that euphemism to their screeches) over a pile of sticks they were clumsily building in a tree that hung over the lake. I have never found a nest since, but as they always visit the feeder less at this time, I assume they are getting more interested in procreating.

I still hear the flying squirrel's surreptitious gnawing most nights. The dogs ignore him now. Last night I sketched him by flashlight. I was surprised to see him curl his tail around the fat pole as an extra grip. I would not have thought that such a weak-looking appendage would have prehensile qualities.

17th March 2005
I have been waiting for the right ice conditions to make a bid for the third lake upriver, which is hard against the Tweedsmuir Provincial Park boundary, and which I therefore call Boundary Lake. It has been warm since my hike to the North Ridge, and travelling any distance is impossible when it is thawing. Today, at last, it was cold enough. A large proportion of the trip would take place on glare ice (which is now quite solid); neither skis nor snowshoes would do well on a surface like that, so I dredged out a pair of crampons I bought years ago when I lived in New Zealand. They were often

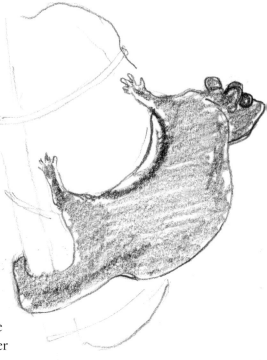

Flying squirrel

needed in the mountains there, but here I have rarely had occasion to use them.

It took me a while to convince my subconscious that I could now stride confidently on the slick surface of the lake, but the crampons gripped perfectly. The snow was so firm on the stretch between the two lakes that I was able to walk on top of it most of the time.

There is not much climbing involved to reach Boundary Lake, just a very gradual rise in altitude. After Cohen Lake (named after the trapper), one passes over a series of swamps that skirt shallow ponds, making it necessary in summer to stick to the side of the valley. But now I could go anywhere and I mostly travelled on the river, which is no more than a couple of paces across at that height.

Despite the lack of elevation gain, Boundary Lake is closer to the coast so receives thirty or forty more centimetres of snow than Nuk Tessli. The country opens up as one approaches the lake, and a different view of the mountains unfolds. Migma, on the right when seen from my window, is now on the left; Pandemonium Pass is in the middle and an unnamed rugged peak is on the right.

Boundary Lake's surface was white and not icy like the other two lakes. A snake of open water by the outlet reflected the cold blue sky. There is something very precious about open water in a frozen landscape. The rocks on the bottom were warm-looking and brown.

There were old otter and wolf tracks along the river, but the only creatures I saw were a couple of mountain chickadees near the old trap cabin at the head of Cohen Lake.

18th March 2005

I picked the right day for my hike to Boundary Lake! Five centimetres of snow and minus 15°C this morning. A nasty east wind is smoking the snow off the roof and driving it into the porch. Even the dogs have barely stirred out of their kennels all day.

The cold snap seems to have encouraged a resurgence of aviary interest in the suet. A Steller's jay battled there this morning, his ragged feathers blowing every which way. When the fat is frozen the birds must whack harder to get a meal. Even the Clark's nutcrackers deigned to visit a couple of times, and at one point the nutcrackers, the two gray jays and the Steller's jay were there at the same time. Three jay species at one feeder—that must be something of a record.

21st March 2005

The equinox! Another few centimetres of snow and minus 12°C again. Finally we are getting more "normal" weather for the time of year. The equinox marks the point where the sun clears Louise O'Murphy when it rises, giving me suddenly a much longer day.

A quick early run around Cranberry Meadows. The river is still roaring despite this cooler spell. The new snow was cold and fluffy and piled on trees like cotton puffs. Windless snow is unusual here; mostly it rides on a blizzard, so the sight was a pretty one. But a southwest wind started about the time I reached the river, and at once the trees plumed with blowing snow. The wind made for a nippy trip back across the lake, and I had to pull my hood over the left side of my face and keep on track using the one uncovered eye.

I couldn't get the internet last night. I thought little of it as it was snowing and the signal does not always come through if the cloud cover is too thick. But I am concerned to find that I still can't raise a signal this morning. Has my system died on me again?

23rd March 2005

The mountains were pink and orange at sunrise, but they were hazed by a veil of snow and they floated serenely over a distant slab of fog. A few snowflakes drifted down by the cabin, the kind that fall as individual crystals, seen in intricate detail through the "wrong" end of the binoculars as they perched on the sleeve of my coat.

I was on my inefficient radiophone to the satellite company for two hours today, and I made another call to Dave Neads, a neighbour fifty kilometres north, who has his own elaborate solar-driven satellite internet. We spent a lot of time running through possible solutions, but no go. (It's very odd using a mouse with one hand and the radiophone transmitter with the other. I am always clicking the wrong thing and wondering why whatever I am trying to do doesn't work.) Too expensive to fly a tech in here—it would have to be by helicopter now. My lake is still fine to land on, but all the places the fixed-wing planes take off from are disintegrating. So Dave's wonderful wife, Rosemary, will check my emails for me and I will try to call her once a week by radiophone. It is not the first time we have had to do this.

24th March 2005

Actually, it's rather fun not having the internet! At first I missed it—it is like watching a soap opera; one gets hooked, wanting to know what happens next. But without it, I have at least an hour a day extra for other things.

Minus 18°C and five centimetres of ice on the waterhole first thing, so I set off to North Pass Lake but had to turn back, as it warmed right up and the sun turned the new snow to gumbo. The birds are beginning to move higher into the forest. I heard mountain chickadees in three places and Clark's nutcrackers in two. I also heard the single call of a pine grosbeak.

They make a low warble that always reminds me of those old bird whistles that you fill with water and blow into. Sometimes pine grosbeaks are around on and off all winter, but this was the first one I have recorded this year. The males are a nice rosy colour, the females more drab.

25th March 2005

The first spring migrants!

There must have been some fog overnight, for patches of hoarfrost were evident; when I woke the almost full moon was backlighting pine needles rimmed with frost fire, and when I skied through Cranberry

Meadows after daylight, the hoar along the river was a centimetre thick.

Where the meadows butt against the river, there is a wide pool that has stayed open for most of the winter. On it were two pairs of mallards. Humble birds indeed, but what a treat to see a fresh sign of life after so many wintery months!

And that was not all. Partway up the river is a shallow bit where the river goes around a bend, and there I heard a clear, beautiful cascade of song that could be only one thing—an American dipper. I did not spot it at first, but as I paused to enjoy a display of fantastic spray icicles

Pine grosbeak

Dipper in icy river

hanging off a fallen log, I saw the drab little bird bobbing on some rocks that poked out of the roiling water.

Usually all they do is make a short, clicking warning call. I have rarely heard them sing here and have assumed they do it only when they are threatening a rival. When I lived at Lonesome Lake (a thousand metres lower), there were generally four or five adults competing for food along the stretch of river in front of my cabin. They were all very vocal; their song is elaborate, full of rich trills and warbles, more reminiscent of a warm summer evening than such frigid surroundings. On the rare occasions that I've heard them perform here, there has always been a second bird. But if there was another one today, I could not find it.

26th March 2005

Dirty-looking fingers of cloud preceded a blank wall of vapour from the west, so the sun was soon swallowed in the murk. A little snow fell, and soon whirling dervishes were marching down the lake in the wind. The temperature was only just below freezing even early in the day and the new snow was slippery as silk, so I fell over quite quickly on my way around The Block.

Near the cabin, red-breasted nuthatches were scrapping and there was a lovely twittery chorus from a group of mountain chickadees. It would seem that three has suddenly become a crowd, and no doubt all sorts of territorial and testosteronic stuff is going on.

27th March 2005
The red squirrel–dog relationship is funny. The squirrel comes frequently throughout the day, and usually, the minute they hear him, the dogs tear around that side of the building and away the squirrel scampers. But every late afternoon he is allowed a prolonged feed—for some reason the dogs let him alone at that hour. The flying squirrel is still visiting at night. He also feeds at peace now, for the dogs no longer bother to get out of bed for him.

3rd April 2005
Minus 4°C first thing so did a quick trip around The Block. Snow was falling for part of the way, big, loose flakes tumbling into stretches of black open water along Otter Creek. Considering how open the creek has been all winter, it is surprising how much ice continues to hang on.

There were a surprising number of tracks all of a sudden. Hares' crossed Cabin Meadow and a ptarmigan's along Otter Creek. Weasel prints were there, too, and again by Lily-less Pond. Nearby was the intricate calligraphy of a deermouse, his trail marked intermittently by his dragging tail. Three pine grosbeaks warbled in the little alley between Salamander and Dandelion meadows.

8th April 2005
After several days of bits of sticky snow and thaw, the stars were brilliant and it was minus 12°C this morning. I could see by the way the dogs were running on the lake that the surface would be hard enough to support skis, so I set off around Cranberry Meadows when it was hardly light. Halfway up the lake to the trailhead, the sun rose and at once my fantastically elongated shadow leapt ahead of me. The skis had monstrously curved tips; my pants were cartoon bellbottoms that tapered to a small trunk with my tiny pinhead of a brain perched on top. The ski poles seemed alive when their shadows shrank and grew as they were raised and lowered.

This early in the day, long-fingered shadows chilled the meadows and nothing seemed to be moving. The only fresh tracks were those of a single hare. But when I arrived back near the cabin, I was enormously surprised to see a northern red-shafted flicker clumsily attempting to get at the fat. Sightings of this bird are as rare as those of the Steller's

Flicker

jay. Is this ridiculously mild winter encouraging these lower-elevation creatures?

9th April 2005

Minus 12°C so a quick early circuit of The Block. I was surprised to see how many bare patches of ground were showing on sunny slopes and in tree wells. They make nice vignettes of winter-scorched vegetation; wide, bleached blades of grasses and sedges, and the dark purple-brown of the dormant Labrador tea. These plants are evergreen and will soon change colour to olive when the sun gets their juices going and photosynthesis starts.

11th April 2005

Juncos! Now this is a real sign of spring—they are the first migratory summer residents.

When I tree-planted for a living, I used to hike out from here on snowshoes during late March or early April. I always looked for the dark-eyed juncos before I left and was never disappointed. One year, when the snow lay deep at the end of March, the juncos didn't hang around—they need open ground to feed—but at least they came. This year, there has been open ground for a month but the juncos are late. Weird.

The juncos like crumbs, but if I toss them onto the snow the dogs lick them up. So yesterday evening, while the dogs were busy with their supper, I scattered crumbs in the clump of slide alders beside the trail to the waterhole. Last year's fallen leaves are poking through the remnants of snow there, and that is where I saw the two birds perching. There was no sign of them at first this morning, but after a failed excursion around The Block (I tried to walk around on boots but kept crashing through the snow so gave up), I was delighted to find their tracks right around the door. They are as companionable as chickens at this time of year. What amazingly long middle toes they have.

Junco and tracks

from a dead
junco 11 Ap 05

12th April 2005

All kinds of excitement!

Minus 10°C and absolutely cloudless first thing. The sunrise colours on the mountain were rich and spectacular. Before the colours faded I was up the lake and headed for Cranberry Meadows.

About half a centimetre of fresh snow showed tracks beautifully. There had been a ptarmigan at the west end of the meadows, and fox tracks followed the old game route through the centre. Both nuthatches and mountain chickadees were calling in several places.

It was chill and shady along the river, and the water's breath had created hoar frost on the overhanging pine branches and alder bushes. Peering through this fairy tracery I observed the dipper on a stone in the river—and then something else flitting secretively through the network of branches. A short tail like a nuthatch, but this was smaller, dark and dumpy. A winter wren! But so fluffed out it was hardly recognizable, just a fuzz ball with a tiny, sharp beak at one end and a ridiculous stub of a tail at the other.

Winter wren

Later, while busy on the computer, I heard an alien *peep peep* and rushed out with the binoculars. A dark, robin-sized bird sat in a tree. A thick bill and a few spots and stripes on its body. Then it moved and revealed red shoulder patches. It was another very rarely seen bird in these parts—a red-winged blackbird. It must have been a subadult male. These birds are very common at Nimpo Lake, where their wonderful *kongarees!* announce the spring, but my visitor only *peeped*.

A not-so-good sight to round off the day was a dead junco at the edge of the deck. Nearby was Bucky, looking sleepily innocent. He is a somewhat rotund dog with short legs so cannot run all that quickly, but he is a very swift killer should something come within reach of his jaws. I once saw him snatch a junco out of the air: three were fighting and whizzing by me almost too fast for me to see; Bucky barely seemed to move and the junco was in his mouth. When bird records are sent in, I am supposed to record any dead ones and if possible give the reason for their demise. It is very embarrassing to have to keep announcing, "The dog ate it."

16th April 2005

Some pretty heavy squalls and flurries these last three days. For once, more is falling than melting—it is the best snow we've had all winter.

I made trips to the head of the lake and again down Cranberry Meadows, but the little flush of bird activity has disappeared. I've noticed before, in both spring and fall, that there is a quick movement of birds just before a storm. My valley runs southwest to northeast. At the southwest end is one of the lowest passes between the great Atnarko/Knot Lake Trench, which has a direct link to the coast, and the interior plateau of the Chilcotin, so flying creatures often migrate through here.

A mountain chickadee was singing its spring song near the cabin. The three-note pattern is similar to that of the black-capped chickadee, but wheezier. At Nimpo Lake both the black-capped and chestnut-backed chickadees live alongside mountain chickadees, but I have seen only the one species here.

18th April 2005

A most pretty effect at sundown yesterday. There was a sudden thick, windless snowfall, with large, soft flakes, enough to whiten all the surfaces again. But it must have been very local as the eastern mountains glowed faintly though it, painted in their sunset colours. Then the cloud thinned but flakes continued to fall from a darkening blue sky. A gorgeous pink band of afterglow remained for a long time behind Louise O'Murphy.

And today was picture perfect. Ribbons of fog dispelled at sunrise, leaving all the bushes white and sparkling with hoar. It got to plus 5°C in the afternoon. Warm enough to sit in an ell on the deck out of the wind. Bare patches have appeared on the ground again and the snow under the eaves on the deck got soft enough to shovel. That is the third time I've cleared it off this year.

19th April 2005

The radio informs me that Vancouver is having a record-breaking hot week, so it is disappointing to see overcast here. It was cool enough indoors to want to keep the stove ticking over, so I was very surprised to see the thermometer recording plus 12°C. Some serious thawing at higher elevations—black rocks have appeared everywhere. The kind of day the birds like to move about in, but I noticed nothing new until sundown when I heard a few bars from—ta-dah—an American robin! No sound is prettier on long, mild spring evenings when the wind has died and the snow is still on the ground.

A large spider ran around my window. Her legs (it must be a "her," as the females are larger) would have reached past the edge of a loonie.

20th April 2005
There was a brief flush of northern lights just before sunrise. It is the first time I have seen them this year. They are always more common in spring and fall and rare in the dead of winter, but the total absence of even a green glow during the last four months was surprising.

Robin

The robin started singing long before it was light enough for me to switch off the lamp. (I can use electric lights now—the days are long enough to give me all the power I need, especially as my internet is out of action.) The robin was still performing after the sun had risen and illuminated his red breast. Another, silent robin was with him, presumably his mate. They don't appear to nest here, usually preferring more open ground higher up the mountains, but they generally give me a pretty decent concert before they leave.

Off early around Cranberry Meadows, where I heard mountain chickadees and nuthatches in various places, and then what I first thought was a robin's warning cry, but when I spotted the orange, black-sashed breasts I knew the birds for varied thrushes.

Varied thrush

Three juncos were also singing in different parts of the meadows. Over the years I have learned that they commence their little concerts about a week after they first arrive. Snowmelt running along the surface of the bogs has started to dissolve the snow from below, and in a number of places I had to slide the skis over the remains of last year's sedge crop and slosh through water.

Up the river I disturbed three spruce grouse, and near the outlet was a group of tiny birds with a high *treeee* call. They were feeding in the tree crowns and flitting so swiftly they were impossible to identify positively, but I am fairly sure they were golden-crowned kinglets. They do not hang about here but merely pass through in spring and fall.

Then the plod across the lake—and darn if there weren't three tree swallows swooping around Kojo's Island, where they usually nest in a snag. What on earth are they finding to eat at this time of year? But they are always among the earliest arrivals, coming when the landscape is still covered in snow and ice.

The temperature reached plus 15°C by the end of the day. Scents so long frozen were suddenly released—the rotten mulch at the river's edge, the gas from the chainsaw sitting idle in the porch, the sun-warmed lichens on the rocks.

Tree swallow

21st April 2005

Things are really starting to move!

Minus 5°C in the morning, plus 14°C in the afternoon. I diligently tried to work on a manuscript for a while, but how can I stay inside in this weather?

I thought I might be able to walk on the lake in just boots, but every few steps I crashed through a crust into ten centimetres of water. So back to the skis; they held me up. They are really noisy when the surface is icy like this. I had hoped to get to Cohen Lake but the portage was too difficult. With skis on, the hummocky country was too slippery, and without them I crashed through to my thighs.

So I simply stood in the sun beside the sparkling river where it runs into my lake and listened. Robins, nuthatches, mountain chickadees, a distant varied thrush and a mystery bird I have heard very occasionally here but never identified. It is the size of a large warbler and, on the rare occasions I have managed to get a look at it, appears to have absolutely no distinguishing marks. Its song is strong and quite deep—five or six *chews*, very slightly descending, followed by a confused trill. I have been calling it the "contralto warbler." For my first dozen years at Nuk Tessli, I never heard it at all, but every summer it is a little bit more common.

Back home, four swallows were checking out nesting sites and a gray jay was collecting scraps of sheep's wool that had leaked out of the dogs' kennels. On the deck it was so hot I had to position myself into the wind to remain comfortable.

Two butterflies appeared—a mourning cloak first and later a northern checkerspot, the latter quite sandy coloured. They are darker in the alpine, which allows them to absorb heat more quickly in the harsher environment. Butterflies cannot move until their body temperature reaches a certain level.

Mourning cloak

Checkerspot

Next arrived a fox sparrow. This is a special bird for me. It has a melodious and distinctive song—*Please don't tell me to take out the trash! Please don't tell me—(giggle giggle).*

It was some years before I identified this bird, having no one to tell me what it was, for it does not sing like this away from the high country. It would greet me as soon as I reached the sixteen-hundred-

Fox sparrow

metre mark on my hike in from the road after tree-planting season, and I have always associated it with my life here. Over the years, however, the fox sparrow's numbers have dropped. I shall be very sorry if they disappear from around my cabins. Half a dozen used to battle it out within earshot of the cabin but now only one, occasionally two, sing.

And while I was sitting there, listening, I was buzzed by a male rufous hummingbird. Robins to hummingbirds in forty-eight hours! That's amazing.

Rufous hummingbird

And then I heard a different buzz. It was a small-engined aircraft. Rosemary had arranged for Floyd, a local pilot, to bring in my mail. He was away all winter and had not put skis on his plane so would not be able to land. He roared low over the cabin to alert me (as if I could miss him!), then turned around and scooted along the ice barely higher than my head. I could see the bulge of a black garbage bag hanging out of the window. The morning's firm crust on the lake had thinned to a window-pane thickness of ice over water—I hoped that the mail was well wrapped. But the drop could not have been more perfect. The bag hit the ice right in front of the buildings and skidded to a slight bump of whiter snow that covered a group of rocks. Floyd buzzed the cabin again and waggled his wings as he swooped over the northeast ridge back to Nimpo.

I put skis on but crashed through into the water anyway. The whiter snow, however, was dry. I grasped my booty and retired to the sun-drenched deck for an orgy of reading. Seven weeks' worth of letters (and bills). Only one item was slightly damaged where a corner of the bag had been abraded; although it had got wet enough to cause the ink to run, the letter was still perfectly legible. I read it first and the opening line had me laughing out loud. It was from a stranger who had written

Golden-crowned sparrow

to comment on one of my books, and she wrote: "I don't know when or how this letter will reach you, but …."

As the sun dropped toward the mountains it grew suddenly quite chilly, so I brought the mail inside. And batting against the window—I had left the door open—was a golden-crowned sparrow.

Spring has not only sprung, it has exploded.

23rd April 2005

I headed off toward the mountains planning to make a day of it, but it was too warm and the mix of ice and rotten snow made progress too slow. At Otter Lake I cut my losses and decided to go around the shore. Where the creek ran into the lake at the upper end, a pool had formed—the last time I had come this way there had been not even a murmur underneath the snow.

There is a similar-sized lake about a kilometre upstream. I'd been up to it only twice before, the first time in summer when the dense brush and boggy, uneven ground made travel difficult, and the second time on snowshoes one March. I thought I might be able to get up there on the snow again. At first I made quite good progress, but just before the next lake the creek did a big dogleg, blocking my way. The creek was wild and roaring; it seemed at first to be wide open all the way along. But where it ran off the steep side of the valley, a tenuous snowbridge spanned the water. The bridge was well down within the creek's vertical walls so I would not be able to get onto it with skis. I took them off and lowered myself cautiously. I had just transferred my full weight onto the bridge when, without a sound, it collapsed and deposited me into knee-deep water. At once the instant agony of numbing feet. The top of the bank was level with my head—no getting out that way, so there was nothing for it but to wade downstream until the water spread and the banks became low enough for me to crawl onto them. But having got there I realized I had lost a pole and had to wade back for it.

24th April 2005

The warmest yet—plus 17°C this afternoon. The mountains were slightly blurred with haze—according to the radio, grass fires are already getting away from people so the haze is probably smoke. With such a low-snow year and dry spring, it looks as though we could be gearing up for another horrific fire season.

At the end of the deck is a small rock garden I built to hide a couple of stumps. It is in a very exposed spot and the winds sweep the snow off it repeatedly throughout the winter, exactly copying the conditions on the high alpine ridges from which I have sneaked a few plants: two draba species, a Jacob's ladder, some grass and a cinquefoil. The last lot of snow has only just gone but all kinds of green bits are appearing. Nothing showed when the ground was bare earlier in winter. Are they responding to the duration of the daylight, or the warmth?

A sudden out-of-the-corner-of-my-eye movement—and there was a yellow pine chipmunk flicking his spindly tail.

Chipmunk

25th April 2005

At last the surface of the ice has firmed up enough so that I can toboggan heavy tools across the lake and do some logging. There are a few useful-looking firewood snags hanging over the water and they are most easily dealt with when the lake is frozen. But when I tackled the first tree, a lodgepole pine that had fallen into the lake at the edge of Corner Island last fall, I realized I had left it almost too late.

I was wearing gumboots so could handle a bit of wet, but a lot of the water close to the dark tree trunk was fully open. I had to do some interesting balancing on bits of firm ice and underwater rocks to buck up the trunk. Before I brought in the chainsaw, I took it well out into the lake and cut straight down. The bar is 65 centimetres long and it did not break through until almost all of it had disappeared.

My robin continues to serenade me every morning, and the juncos and chickadees are singing lustily. Yellow-rumped warblers have now joined the chorus, and a ruby-crowned kinglet is just beginning to warm up his repertoire. *Chubby chubby chubby cheek cheek cheek chubby chubby chubby chubby cheek!* They are such cheerful-sounding birds. Sometimes they get stuck on the *chubby* part like a broken record.

Another hummer whizzed by, attracted by the red chainsaw. Two hummers don't make a summer, but I figure it is time to put up a feeder.

And later, while I was preparing supper, through the open door came—a mosquito!

Yellow-rumped warbler

Ruby-crowned kinglet

26th April 2005

It has suddenly become impossible to get to the waterhole. These last warm days the water level has risen and a large area around the hole is awash. It is now easier to haul what I need from a small space that has melted near one of the rocks by the shore. There is no room for the bucket, so I must take a small pot along and scoop the water out. The pool is covered with a fine film of scum that must be pushed away and the pot dipped in quickly before the scum can flow back. Melting snow is not an option—that would be even worse, being full of needles and bits of bark, not to mention dog hair, or worse. The lake water will do me no harm if I boil it. It's probably a lot better than city water even so.

Beyond the uncertain conditions along the shore, the ice surface is now perfectly solid. I loaded the chainsaw, gas, chain oil, tools and a lunch onto the toboggan, strapped crampons to my boots and set off kitty-corner across the lake to where Big Inlet jogs back. This inlet is really just an underwater extension of Cranberry Meadows. A small group of pines there have turned red, victims of the mountain pine beetle.

This insect has received a lot of publicity recently, as the worst infestation in recorded history has browned an enormous area in the north and centre of the province. People have forgotten that a big wave came into this area about twenty years ago and everyone was crying *Plague!* then. But it went away of its own accord. Logging companies enjoy this brouhaha as they can cut many more trees than would normally be allowed. Only pockets of infection entered my area twenty years ago, and those snags close to the shore have been very useful to me for both building and firewood. The current wave reached Nimpo Lake a couple of years ago, and the first dead trees appeared on my lake last fall.

Pine beetle

The rice grain–sized beetle hatches in ambient temperatures of 16°C. The mature female bores a hole in a tree, at the same time releasing a pheromone to attract the male. Both partners excavate a vertical channel in the cambium layer, with side channels branching off it. The cambium layer is the main cell factory of the tree: new bark is formed on the outside and new timber cells emerge from the inside. These timber cells are hollow and stacked end to end so that they can transport water and nutrients into the tree, and they form the sapwood. As they age, they fill up with lignum and turn into the heartwood that gives the tree its strength.

The beetle's eggs are laid and fertilized. When the larvae hatch, they eat. If the larvae occur in large numbers, the simple act of chewing will destroy enough of the cambium layer to damage the tree. But the insect carries another threat: a fungus, which, if present in sufficient quantities, blocks the sapwood cells and destroy the tree's plumbing, thus giving the beetle greater freedom of movement. It is the fungus that causes the characteristic blue stain found in beetle-killed trees. It dwells inside the insect's body without harming it, ready to be passed on to the next generation.

The beetle has proved to be impossible to control; once the telltale red needles appear, the insect is long gone. Young healthy trees usually drown the infestation with resin, but when the insect is this prolific, mature or stressed trees succumb. The recent drought years, exacerbated by poor logging practices, have contributed to the beetle's spread, although one of the main reasons for this current plague is said to be the necessity to extinguish forest fires combined with our recent mild winters. In warm weather, naturally occurring forest fires keep beetle populations down. In cold weather, the pupae overwintering in the bark of trees are apparently killed off by 40-below spells in winter and prolonged 25-below periods in the spring, conditions that we have not had for several years.

Both species of pine in my area, lodgepole and whitebark, are affected by the beetle. Lodgepole is a very strong tree for a softwood; whitebark is exceedingly weak. Lodgepole burns much hotter than whitebark, but I am not picky about which trees I take for wood, leaving only those that have too much spiral to split.

This day I felled three lodgepoles. One of them was a pretty good size for this part of the world, maybe sixty centimetres through. It had a bit of butt rot but that was nothing unusual. Unfortunately, the part of the lake into which it fell was already partially open, and the crash as the tree came down did nothing to improve the situation underfoot.

The other two trees were smaller and the ice was better underneath. I bucked those two and tossed the log rounds high on the shore in the hope that they would land clear of the high-water mark—not that I anticipated much of a flood in this dry year.

Then I started on the big one. The butt rot ended after a couple of rounds, but to my chagrin I ran into red rot almost immediately. It was one of the worst cases I had ever seen—almost the whole interior of the tree was a sponge. The initial stages of the disease turn the heartwood red, but in advanced cases the cells are filled with the white mycelium of the fungus that causes it. I cut a few twisted rounds off the upper branches but soon ran into the rot again. This was a real nuisance.

Not only had I gone through the angst of falling (I still hate doing it, even after twenty-five years) with very little to show for it, I now had a monstrous rotten hulk with a chainsaw cut at either end defacing that part of the shore. I would have to get rid of it, but because of the open water underneath I would have to leave it until the water in the lake had dropped. There is over a metre's difference between high water and low water on this lake. A lot of the shallow area that was already thawed under the tree would be dry land by the middle of summer. I could buck it up then and drag it back into the bush to hide it.

There are a few more trees that I intend to log, but tomorrow I'm going to use this good ice for fun.

27th April 2005

Off at fox sparrow song yesterday (not quite as early as the robin, though) in an effort to get to Boundary Lake and back before travel became too difficult. I figured I could get away with hiking boots alone

Bald eagle on nest

for the ice—which now had a slightly granular surface and would get slushy later in the day—but dragged the snowshoes in the toboggan for the spaces between the lakes.

There is an eagles' nest near the head of my lake, and I was surprised to see the female sitting like a duck on it.

It's not the way one normally pictures eagles, but of course how else could they incubate their eggs? She seemed unperturbed by me with my grating toboggan and the dogs running around beneath, but eyed us with interest. The only time I've ever seen young raised at this nest was last year: I didn't think it was possible for eagles to breed two years in a row.

The creek was very full where it ran into the lake, and a greyer water stain spread for quite a way into the ice. I gave it a wide berth. A breezy northeast wind was ruffling the open water of the river and wavelets sparkled against the sky-reflected blue. How fresh and clean water looks when it runs beside the ice.

Going through the portage was hell! Sloping ice for one step, rotten snow the next, all mixed with a tangle of brush, rocks and fallen logs. But the distance is not far, and soon I was striding over the ice of Cohen Lake. It is smaller than mine, both narrower and shorter, and also shallower. It freezes a month earlier some years. The surface had quite a different texture from that of my lake, being smoother and greyer.

The stretch between Cohen and Boundary lakes is a great deal longer than the portage, but it proved to be a lot easier to negotiate. After the first piece of forest, I moved onto glazed flat snow covering the shallow ponds and meadows. The snowshoes clattered awkwardly on the hard surface, but without them I broke through once in a while so kept them on.

Green-winged teal (female)

Below a small section of rapids, some of the bank snow had fallen into the creek, and standing on a lump of it was a tiny, rotund speckled duck. It was smaller than a mallard but that was the extent of my identification until her partner paddled out from behind the fallen chunk. He was most splendidly attired in a dark reddish cap and a wide purple-green iridescent stripe running laterally over his eye and forming a crest at the back of the head. White vertical

Green-winged teal (male)

slashes at the shoulder and the rear of his body bracketed greyish, slightly speckled flanks.

When the dogs came close to the bank, he raised his crest a little and uttered wheezy squawks. I had not seen these birds before and had not brought my field guide, so I would just have to remember the details.

Just above this point, beaver had dammed the creek many years ago. They periodically move up into this country when it becomes too crowded downriver, but there is not enough feed for them and they usually die out during the winter. This particular group must have been active for a while, though, because the dam had flooded a vast expanse, killing several mature lodgepoles that now litter the area as grey snags. It is a haven for hole-nesting birds and I have seen tree swallows and flickers breeding here in the past, although neither bird was visible today. Beneath the snow lie large mudflats only partially grown over with sedges.

Where the creek runs out of Boundary Lake there was quite a large stretch of open water. It was inhabited by several Barrow's goldeneyes. This is one of the few ducks I am familiar with. I encounter them every summer and have even seen hatchlings up in the alpine. The handsome dark purple and white males disappear after mating, so usually only the brown-headed, grey-bodied female is the caregiver. (The ducklings are like something out of Walt Disney—black with chubby white cheeks and a perfect Donald Duck profile.)

At my end of the stretch of open water, four goldeneye females sat

Barrow's goldeneyes

like wallflowers at a country dance, but at the farthest edge of the pool, two pairs swam companionably together. Each pair did an occasional head-bobbing routine, not only up and down but also from side to side. Usually each bird performed alone, but occasionally a pair was charmingly synchronized. I guess that's what passes for foreplay in the Barrow's goldeneye world.

The clean water sparkled between brilliant banks, the sun poured from a cerulean sky and the mountains were reflected in the pool. Fox sparrows and ruby-crowned kinglets were singing and a grouse boomed faintly in the distance, whether a spruce grouse or a blue grouse I did not know. Their sound is very similar and at this location it could be either.

Going home, I had to travel into the wind and it was decidedly chilly; the snow, however, was quickly disintegrating. I reached Cohen Lake in reasonable time, but then had a setback. The rink-smooth ice now had a thin film of water on top and could not have been more slippery. Why on earth did I not have the sense to bring the crampons?

The Vibram soles of my hiking boots are hopeless in these conditions, and even the snowshoe webs gave no grip at all. I crept along, centimetre by centimetre, often skidding sideways on the small bumps that textured the surface. It was going to take hours to get down the lake at this rate. Just about the point where I was as far away from land as I could be, I decided I had to try something different—socks. I was wearing my only good pair, the set I was saving for long-distance travel; all my others had holes, patches or darns in them. There was nothing for it but to take off my boots and stuff them under the snowshoes in the toboggan. At last I could move a little faster than a geriatric snail. It wasn't too cold except where tiny hollows had collected water. I headed to the nearest shore; a bit of snow ice ran intermittently along the edge of the lake, and this provided just enough traction to put my red boots back on.

As I left the lake, I ran into wolf tracks. The animal had not always been successful in staying on top of the snow—I could see how he had splayed his toes as my dogs do in an effort not to crash through. The tracks must have been pretty fresh. In this thawing time, prints become distorted and often disappear within hours. If the wolf had passed by before I had come along, he would have stayed on top of the snow. So he was likely not too far away.

It was now mid-afternoon, far later than I had expected to be returning through the portage, and it was awful. Every time I flopped through the snow, which was at almost every step even with the snowshoes on, I fell over to the front, sideways and backward. But my lake, when I finally reached it, was not too bad at all. The surface was a grey sludge; I often broke through into water, but it was not so slippery. Then I was nearly defeated just getting off the ice, for the band of open water I had jumped across with ease first thing in the morning had widened considerably. The shore drops off steeply there and I did not fancy getting wet above the knee, so I had to hunt up and down the shore until I found a safer place to get onto dry land.

My beautiful little tubby ducks are green-winged teal; they are apparently very common but I have not seen them before.

29th April 2005

Minus 4°C to plus 4°C, so much colder yesterday. I skied around Cranberry Meadows, but it was disappointing as far as wildlife was concerned. The river could be heard a kilometre away, and beside it I could hear nothing else.

Trees thickly overhang the trail beside the river and prevent much snow from accumulating on it. But the sun pokes underneath, and now large patches of bare ground cover the route. I took the skis off and had the wonderful pleasure of walking on soft, aromatic, silent duff.

Three gray jays came to the feeder, all fluffed out with cold. I heard a distant flicker.

1st May 2005

Mayday! Mayflowers! Maypoles! But not here. I did see the first open flower, though.

Pussy willow

May 1st 2005

Salix sp. ♂

Salix lucida ♀

It was the pussy willow I first saw with its silvery buds on March 10th. Today a few stamens were poking out from the dense, silvery pelts. The stamens are yellow but the unopened staminate flowers are bright red, so the composite flower is quite colourful. I still don't know which species it is.

It was my day for calling Rosemary on the radiophone, but it took some time to get through. This often happens when there is cloud or fog or frost on the repeater, which there probably is today. She says that the ice at Nimpo Lake went out a few days ago, supposedly two weeks early although I've known it go in April before. Down at the Precipice, where Rosemary lives, they are coping with major flooding. It's the same on the Chilcotin, too. Puddles and holes that have been dry for decades are full of water, and the mess of mud and receding ice is apparently unbelievable.

3rd May 2005

A calm, clear morning, so off early for a trip around Cranberry Meadows. Getting on and off the lake required some care, even with skis on. This day's new sight was a pair of common mergansers on the big pool below the rapids.

Common mergansers

essli I never encountered these birds, and
, by Wayne Campbell, et al., states they
ations above twelve hundred metres. But
Nuk Tessli lies at nearly sixteen hundred
d females with young on two or three
anding their range. As with the Barrow's
ing, and after mating they leave the drab
while they go off on their summer-long

e only regular
other birds
ld food. In
sun poured
low, a male
ing to get at a
over that I had left
not far away and
but it was the
in love with.

To North Pass Lake! Predictably difficult going up on the icy snow through the forest and hell coming back through the softened rot, but above the forested area and away from the trees it was perfect.

There was quite a bit more bare ground along Otter Creek than on the first of this month, although I still needed the skis; a few more days will make a big difference there, I think. It was quite tricky to get onto Otter Lake as the pool above the outlet has spread considerably. A pair of Barrow's goldeneyes was in temporary residence.

Edith Meadow (named after my mother—the first time I saw it, it was full of flowers and my immediate thought was: I wish my mother could see this) had a wide swath open down the middle. All kinds of green spikes were showing, mostly of leather-leaved saxifrages and sedges. Leather-leaved saxifrages are evergreen, but the old growth is drab and the new growth is much lighter and softer. A ruby-crowned kinglet and a yellow-rumped warbler had staked their claims to this little pocket of sunshine. Otherwise, nothing much was moving through the forest—except a surprising number of mosquitoes, which were quite a pest as I could not travel fast enough to escape them—I had never dreamed that a net might be useful so early in the year. Above the Steep Bit, the route veers west over country that is mostly open and full of running bog holes in summer but was nice and white and smooth now. Judging by the tree wells, there was still at least a metre of snow on the ground. The first meadow hosted a robin (it always has one), another kinglet, another yellow-rumped warbler and two fox sparrows. One of these had quite a different call. There is always some variation with these birds' songs, but this one's was very much abbreviated. *Please don't tell me NO!* The same short phrase repeated over and over. Less than half a "normal" song. How do the females react to these differences? Probably not well, otherwise there would be more dramatic variations.

At the beginning of this open area was another tiny piece of bare bog. In it, a couple of globe flowers and mountain marsh marigolds were already opening their petals even though the flowerheads had barely cleared the ground. Both species are common at high altitudes in these sodden conditions. They are designed to bloom the minute the snow goes. They must react to the strengthening light through the thinning pack; I have seen them at times with their flowers wide open under several roaring centimetres of swollen creek. These specimens looked a little beat up, as if the cold had been too much for them.

Globe flower and mountain marsh marigold

While I was admiring them, a greyish-bluish bird flitted onto a nearby willow. Quite drab at a distance, it proved, through the binoculars, to be a yellow-rumped warbler. Magnified by the lenses, the neon-bright yellow flashes on rump, sides and throat were brilliant. One almost gets the feeling they are overdoing it.

6th May 2005

I expected to be able to ski up the lake to check on the eagles' nest today but the surface was so precarious I turned back. No doubt there is plenty of solid ice at the bottom, but beneath the thin surface skin is a good thirty centimetres of water. I avoided the greyest places, but even so I could feel the ice bending at times. It's no fun when you expect to fall in at every step. There is only one place left where I can get on and off the lake near the cabins, and that will go momentarily,

Yellow-rumped warbler

so it looks as though my ice-walking days are over for this year.

I got far enough to see the large crescent of open water that has formed where Otter Creek runs into the lake. Two Canada geese stood on the ice nearby. They seemed reluctant to fly and merely flapped and flopped until they reached the water. They are never very common here. Parties of three or four fly around in spring and fall, and I sometimes run into them in summer on higher, shallow lakes, where they congregate in small groups to shed their flight feathers.

A couple of woodpeckers have been active among the tree trunks around the cabin recently. They have been gone for a while so it is nice to have them back. They whistle shrilly to each other as they scrabble up the flaky bark, and there has been some quite dramatic drumming.

7th May 2005

Plus 2°C first thing and there seemed to be a bit of fog when I looked out of the window in the half dark, but daylight revealed a lightly falling snow. Despite the cloudy day, the snow soon thawed off the bare patches of ground, which are now considerable on the sunny side of the cabin. I can go down naked rock steps to my now very big waterhole by the rocks and no longer need to chop it open, although there is usually a network of ice crystals on it first thing. Soon it will be possible to start washing heavy stuff like blankets—not only because quantities of water will be easily accessible, but also because the blankets will dry outside. The whole cabin is in desperate need of a spring clean.

The trail to the outhouse is disintegrating with very little trouble. Some years it develops a big slope as the sunny side melts faster than the shady side, and I often slip off it into the deep, soft stuff alongside. At other times the trail rots and I must don the snowshoes. But this year it has simply flattened to thin sheets of ice that can be levered away. Only one small area still has snow on it. I can now safely dispense with the creepers I have worn since March on the bottoms of my boots. There never has been a year like it for ice.

8th May 2005

Heard a loon! I should imagine that there is now quite a big pool at the head of the lake where the river comes in. I wonder if the open water has reached the eagles' nest yet. When it gets big enough, the wind will start working at the ice and that will help break it up.

A second fox sparrow was singing this morning by the cabin. The two birds seem to sing in a coordinated manner, one waiting for the other to finish before it starts. Duets like these used to be common.

Three geese landed in front of the west window on the ice. Right where I turned back the other day. *They* didn't sink.

9th May 2005

Open ground is appearing on all the south-facing slopes, and I figured that if I could reach Otter Creek, which runs into the lake close to where the shore was well exposed to the sun, I should have a pretty clear trail as far as Big Beach. The section between Cabin Meadow and Otter Creek was shady, and there was still a lot of snow, but by climbing windfalls and ducking branches, I gained the open ground. The pool at the foot of the creek was inhabited by pairs of Barrow's goldeneyes, mallards and common mergansers.

I didn't get right onto Big Beach, as a normally tiny creek that probably created the beach in the first place was too deep and wild to cross without getting wet feet. Not far beyond, the shore did another jog—south this time—and that section of shore was full of snow. Which meant I could not get close to the eagles' nest anyway. But through the binoculars I could make out a white head in the right position for a sitting bird so assume they are still incubating.

The tiny creek had created a surprisingly large open pool beside the beach. It was tenanted by three male and two female goldeneyes. They arranged themselves most photogenically on a perfect reflection of Flat Top Mountain; unfortunately they were a bit too far away for the camera. But I enjoyed sitting there and looking at them while I ate my sandwich. All of a sudden there was the oddest noise—a sort of hollow *whoosh,* but quite faint and over so quickly I was not sure whether I had imagined it. But the next moment, in scooted two more pairs of goldeneyes. At once there was much head-bobbing and lunging accompanied by a hoarse *yank,* not unlike that of a red-breasted nuthatch but much deeper—a baritone compared with the nuthatch's alto. Despite the status shuffling, which went on for about ten minutes, they all stayed in a tight group even though there was plenty of water all around them.

On the way home I stumbled upon the fourth open flower of the year—a soopolallie or soap berry, so called because the berries are full of saponins that make a froth when the fruit is stirred up.

First Nations people have always enjoyed them but many others find them bitter. I have grown to like them and nibble the few ripe ones I find. They are absolutely delicious after a frost, but they are ready early and the bears also love them, so I do not often find them in that delectable state.

This plant was male—there seem to be considerably more male than female bushes at this altitude (which is close to the edge of their range). The flower is tiny and petalless, consisting of four lime green sepals and a bunch of stamens in a little tuft. The female flower has a single ovary. The plant has the distinction of being the only indigenous species to have no protective bracts for its emerging foliage. The buds, two leathery-looking olive leaves clasped like praying hands, emerge in the fall and are able to winter in that state. The flowers grow right in the axils of the leaves, and their buds are little round balls that crowd in bunches like grapes. Open, they are a little froth of greenish yellow. If the soopolallies were out, I reasoned, maybe the crowberries were blooming, too.

soopolallie

Some searching among sunnier clumps at the bases of trees produced these even tinier, barely visible flowers. Like soopolallie blossoms, they are pared down to essentials: three bracts (which would have formed the bud), three stamens and a single pistil.

Crowberry

11th May 2005

On my way down to the lake to fetch water, there was a sudden *whoosh* and a pair of common mergansers zoomed around the shore at chest height, no more than two metres away.

I don't know who was more startled, them or me. One doesn't realize how big these birds are until they are close by. They are very swift and streamlined fliers. They veered across the lake and landed near

Flying common mergansers

the outlet pool, touching down quite far into the lake—I could see the splash of water (I wear binoculars every waking moment at this time of year). I keep hearing noises from that direction and am sure there are all sorts of interesting visitors, but I can't cross the lake, and going round the shore would be a major chore as I would have to traverse a long, shady stretch of snow. It is most frustrating, but I surely shouldn't have to wait too much longer for the lake to be open.

12th May 2005

There was so much bare ground along Otter Creek when I went to the North Pass a week ago that I thought I might be able to do The Block without skis. Water would probably be my biggest problem, so gumboots were the footwear of choice. I have one pair of town shoes but five different kinds of boots for this life of mine—hiking boots, gumboots, ski boots, and two pairs of felt-lined boots, one with creepers on, and then there are the snowshoes, skis and crampons. Right now I need something different on my feet almost every day.

I love walking the trails when they are newly emerged from the snow. Littered with the winter's accumulation of pine needles, they are clean and sweet and blend with the forest as if they had appeared spontaneously. Later they will become dusty and marked with footprints that are not my own.

Hermit thrush

Cabin Meadow was almost bare and totally waterlogged. A new bird for the year was singing in it—a hermit thrush.

This is another species that has got thinner on the ground since I have lived here: now I may hear one or two within earshot of the cabin, whereas before there were half a dozen. The hermit thrush has been described as having one of the most beautiful and haunting songs in the bird world, but there seems to be a lot of regional variation and here it merely sounds squeaky. The introductory note is quite short compared with that of other areas. *Dee—diddly dee,* on a slightly descending scale, then a repeat at a lower pitch.

Otter Lake looked fairly solid, but I wasn't about to experiment. A lone male Barrow's goldeneye cruised the pool. A second hermit thrush sang near there, joined by a kinglet, a yellow-rumped warbler and a varied thrush.

Five small ponds are scattered along the meadows that lead down to the shore of my lake; three of these were open, and in one were two incipient pond-lily pads, still underwater, pushing up like vertical rolls of parchment from the sludgy bottom. In a sunny spot among the sedges, five mountain marsh marigolds were blooming, their stalks a couple of centimetres high.

Near home, a raven was perched on the ice. Ravens and crows are never common here—I think this one must have found a sliver of discarded dog bone.

Loon

14th May 2005

Dull this morning, with racing clouds promising wind and the thermometer registering plus 6°C. For the first time, the delicate skin of ice that has been forming every night on newly exposed water, even when there has been no frost recorded on the thermometer, was absent.

For days I have been watching the erratic band of open water running north along the shore toward Crescent Island, and at last I figured it was worth trying to launch a canoe. Not a great day weatherwise for such a momentous event, but it is so exciting to have the feel of the water again. The channel was barely wider than the boat, and because the shore twisted and turned, I continuously grated against ice. It looked about as strong and waterlogged as wet toilet paper, but there was no way I could go through it. The inlets were frozen so I had to creep along the edge there, too. The water is getting close to the highest point for this year—it is always at its maximum when the ice goes out—and many rocks that are normally visible lurked below the surface so I had a bit of manoeuvring to do to avoid these.

To my surprise, once I got around the end of Crescent Island I could see that the far two-thirds of the lagoon was wide open. No wonder I kept hearing waterbird noises. A Canada goose and a male mallard were keeping each other company at the far end, and a lone loon swam at the nearer one.

Ice solidly spanned the distance between us and progress that way was blocked, but the shore and slope behind it are exposed to the sun so it was completely devoid of snow. I parked the canoe and climbed up to a rock where I knew there would be a good view up the lake. I thought I might be able to see some open water, but there is still a lot of ice out there. As far as I can make out, the open area from the inlet has not even reached Eagle Point. I was too far away to see if the nest is still tenanted.

Once I was home, the expected wind got up, quite gusty at times. A good day to concentrate on manuscript work, and I became so absorbed in what I was doing I did not notice that dramatic changes were happening on the lake. Toward the western mountains, the ice seemed as solid as ever, but beyond the bay window, large cracks had formed, one of them between my wharf and Big Island. The shore where I had canoed just hours before was now completely shut in; broken plates of ice had been pushed right up onto the rocks. I was looking at a miniature model of the earth's tectonic plates, breaking apart, smashing into and crumpling and riding over each other—except there weren't any volcanoes in the gaps!

15th May 2005

The wind quit during the night but the cloud level thickened soon after first light, and then it started raining. A real spring rain. Later a wild squall started and I could hear the sibilant tinkling of the grating and disintegrating ice as the plates moved back and forth. I think I can see open water at the far end of the lake, but I've been fooled before: I've often looked at dark areas with binoculars, but heat waves dance off the ice and everything shimmers so it is difficult to make out the difference between solids and liquids. The ice has jammed against the shore below

Gulls

the cabin and it is now very difficult to get water again, as the tiny gaps open to me are choked with pine needles.

Two gulls appeared—glaucous-winged, I think. They simply hung there on the wind while I split wood below.

16th May 2005

Every time I wake I wonder if the ice will still be there, but it always is.

A little clearer this morning with some gleams of orange light on the mountains that were startlingly reflected in the thin ribbons of open water.

Two pairs of large ducks were resting at the edge of a pool not far from my bay window. Their heads were tucked into their wings and the light was not good, but rectangles of rich red on the sides of the males, and green on what I could see of their heads, indicated northern shovelers. I have recorded these aptly named birds only once before, so that was quite a coup.

shovelers

A trail runs through the viewpoint I visited the other day and continues over much higher bluffs that have much better views toward the head of the lake. I figured I should be able to get a good handle on the ice situation from there. An unexpected bonus was the kinnikinnick. It was blooming profusely and had smothered the bluffs with little pink bells. Kinnikinnick is an amazing ground-cover shrub that grows just as happily along the coast as in the alpine. While admiring them I thought

Kinnikinnick and bee

I could hear a distant plane—sometimes the sound of high-altitude jets is deflected down from their pathways across the heavens. But the gentle drone was the wild bumblebees working the blossoms.

Several soopolallie bushes were also blooming among the rocks. Willows, blackberry, huckleberries and mountain azalea all showed green tips to their buds, and a straggling knee-high saskatoon bush (it never grows any taller here) was almost in full leaf, displaying that beautiful spring bronzy green of lower-elevation deciduous trees that is seen so rarely here.

As I climbed higher, I looked up the lake eagerly—but wouldn't you know it, the top end was hidden by a thick band of fog! So I still couldn't see how far the open water had progressed, although no doubt the fog had been created by just that. Flat Top and Monarch sailed like ships above the grey band, and flashes of blue from the partially clouded sky were reflected in the open leads near the cabin.

More wind during the afternoon, this time accompanied by rain, hail, snow and sleet. Now I can definitely see a strip of water up the lake from the cabin.

I really thought the ice would go out once the wind started to blow, but it didn't!

17th May 2005

Surely this will be the day!

But at first light it was minus 2°C and I was surprised to see snowflakes glinting briefly close to the window in the light of the lamp. Daylight revealed only a skiff on the ground, but the ice was all white, including the open leads, which must have frozen over again. The water is still pretty cold out there.

Because of the ever-larger patches of bare ground around the cabins, my low-elevation excursions are no longer dependent on frost. So I gumbooted round The Block in the afternoon for a change. All the ponds in the meadows were open. The pond-lily plants were well developed, many with their pads beginning to spread on the surface. Incipient flowers were mostly underwater still, manifest as round knobs on the ends of vertical stalks.

The water surface around the plants was alive with water striders and crazy beetles.

How do they winter? As adults? Or do they have to hatch? The light-haloed shadows of the water striders' feet—or, more accurately,

Crazy beetles

the shadows of the dimples they create in the water's meniscus, always remind me of Mickey Mouse—the two large ones like round ears, and the smaller ones like eyes. (That is the second time I have anthropodisneyized the wildlife: shows where my artistic upbringing started.)

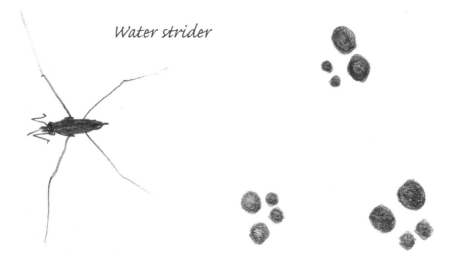

Water strider

It was quite a novelty to have an afternoon hike and see the different way the sunlight dappled the forest and smell the sun-warmed needles. Otter Lake was still largely frozen, my old ski tracks visible as strange hieroglyphs reminiscent of the giant Nazca drawings in the coastal deserts of Peru.

18th May 2005

By yesterday afternoon the new ice had thawed and the plates began to move again, but very slowly. The wind had backed to the southeast, and when the sun went behind the supper tree, a broad band of water appeared in front of my cabin, although the ice still looked solid through the west window. During the night most of the ice up the lake disappeared, but I am still fenced in by a band that links the islands surrounding the cabin. There was plenty of open water toward Crescent Island, however, and I was soon out in the canoe again to see what I could see. It was dull and windless; two loons and two mergansers were on the lagoon; a fox sparrow was singing on Crescent Island, and I heard a distant ruby-crowned kinglet and a varied thrush.

I was aiming for the outlet so I could walk down the river to the pool below the rapids. What interesting visitors had I missed since the last time I was able to ski that way? The water was roaring where it tipped out of the lake, and the licking waves were only a few centimetres below the two-log bridge I built three years ago.

If any birds were singing along the river I could not hear them above the roaring water. The pool at the bottom of the rapids was no longer a restful place but full of roiling current, so it was not too surprising to find it untenanted as well.

Walking up Cranberry Meadows would have been an unpleasant slog among tussocks and waterlogged ground, so I contented myself with creeping along the edge beside the river. Only a small band of snow was left, tucked along the shady side. Beside it was the first sandpiper of the year. Spotted, solitary and semipalmated sandpipers have been observed here, but apart from the spotted, I rarely know which is which unless I am lucky enough to get a really close look.

The dogs were having a wonderful time, noses down and bums in the air, investigating what I thought were flooded-out mouse nests and tunnels that had been made under the snow and now wriggled all over the sodden meadow. But a V-shaped ripple in an area of standing water heading away from the dogs proved to be the wake of what I assumed was a lemming, so the nests were not yet abandoned. The creature was short tailed with grey flanks, and bigger than the little red-backed voles I sometimes catch in the attic. The dogs had not noticed it, so I called them away and returned to the canoe.

I spent the afternoon doing outside chores and when I thought to look at the lake again, all the ice had moved back to my side! There didn't seem to be much wind, and the ice just sat there.

Right at sundown the clouds began to break a little and a brisk wind sprang up. Beyond the ring of ice, the surface of the lake was wind-furred; behind it the water barely rippled. But within half an hour, the ice simply vanished. I was lulled to sleep by a sound I had not heard for so long—the little slap of wavelets on the rocks.

20th May 2005

I was all excited about going up the lakes as soon as the ice went, but these last two days have been gloomy and wildly windy. So I had to content myself with tramps around The Block. The water has dropped ten centimetres already. In a sunny spot, several pink candy-like buds and a single fully out flower of the swamp laurel were showing. These unusual and beautiful buds have two knobs on the outside of each petal; these are pockets designed to hold the anthers. They make the buds look like little cones of cake frosting. As the flower opens, the anthers stay locked, the filaments become spring loaded: touched by a fly, they

swamp laurel

bounce up and wallop the visitor with pollen.

Lilyless Pond is so named because it is the only one in the area where pond-lilies do not grow—and yet it appears to be the same depth and temperature as the others. I have even tried transporting seeds, to no effect. The pond was populated by some tiny, black crescent-shaped larvae hanging below the surface. Hundreds stay suspended as if on strings, one below the other. They are there every year but I have never managed to figure out what they hatch into.

Things are starting to happen in the forest, too. On the far side of Otter Creek's upper bridge the first yellow round-leaved violets were out.

There was no sign of their blossoms when I came this way two days ago. Farther down the trail the spore producing shoots of the running club moss were already full of pollen. Flicking them with my finger caused a puffy yellow explosion.

Round-leaved violet

21st May 2005
Finally, to Boundary Lake!

A bit of snow fell in the late dark, but there was no wind and the clearing sky promised a kinder day. As the wind would most certainly get up later, I was back into early mode. Mount Monarch was newly painted with snow at sunrise when I set off, and pink-washed bits of it were poking up above a band of vapour.

At last I could get a good look at the eagles' nest. A bird was still sitting (both parents share in the incubating). What an exposed position they have. The storms seem bad enough when I am sheltered inside my cabin, but the nest is near the top of one of the tallest trees in the area and right in the wind funnel between the two lakes. There is always a little enclave of activity around the portage. The birds must like the early open water and thickly brushed banks. Along that short stretch I could hear a kinglet, a yellow-rumped warbler, two hermit thrushes, a mountain chickadee and a robin.

I built the portage not long after I first came here, paving the hundred metres with short logs lying crosswise so I can pull a canoe from one end to the other. None of this testosteronic hauling canoes on one's head for me! It is a shady spot so there were still patches of snow, which made the walking harder but the pulling easier.

You can't see into Cohen Lake until you pass through another pool, and the view this morning was absolutely breathtaking. The lake was as smooth as glass, and the mountains poking out of their now quite solid-looking clouds were perfectly mirrored in it. Although it was windless on the water, puffs of grey cloud moved swiftly overhead so that various points along the shore stood out as lit or unlit, constantly changing, adding to the patterns in the reflections. A band of ice almost crossed the lake near the outlet, and I had to do some dodging about to get through it, so I wouldn't have been able to get up the lakes any sooner than today even if the weather had cooperated.

I had seen two loons on my lake, and there was another pair on this one. Four is the usual number between the two bodies of water throughout the summer. But I rarely see evidence of them breeding; I have observed young ones only three times in eighteen years. Near the derelict trap cabin at the head of the lake, the "contralto warbler" was singing lustily. I pursued it for a while but never got a good look at it.

The hiking trail to Boundary Lake is a new one. I joined bits of the trapper's old horse trail to stretches I made from scratch. Near the beginning was a small section that needed brushing out. I had brought the clippers with me, but that was a waste of time as a huge patch of snow covered a wide area there. I had to make quite a detour to get around it and even then I had to flounder through part of the drifts. In one place old wolf tracks stitched a blurry pattern across the needle-freckled snow. There is nothing like this amount of snowpack left anywhere near my cabins—it just shows how much more snow falls even this short distance west.

It was such hard work that I almost gave up but figured if I could reach the open spaces, travel would be better. Most of the ground even there was still covered, and where I had slogged on snowshoes before there were now wide stretches of open water. The snow was pretty firm, though, and I was able to walk more or less normally. Boundary Lake, although it had sported such a large outlet pool when last I came, was still a third frozen. The towers of cloud had grown while I had been hiking; now they hid the mountains.

Here as everywhere else, the concentration of birds was now less. This is particularly noticeable with the ducks; presumably new niches are opening higher up. One female and two male goldeneyes in the open part of Boundary Lake and three common mergansers along the river were all the waterbirds I saw. I heard a flicker and saw a glimpse of the red underwing across the water. A new bird for the year was an olive-sided flycatcher. Fortunately it has a very distinctive call: *Whup THREE beers!* (although the *whup* is not always audible), so it is easy to identify among what can otherwise be a very difficult family to differentiate. There seemed to be a lot of juncos about, some in pairs and some single, but none of them sang. They are such self-important little guys with their tubby bodies and their smart black waistcoats.

Three or four sandpipers were present; I saw only two but heard the others.

23rd May 2005

I picked the right day to go up the lake! The last two have been unpleasantly cold and windy with a bit of falling snow.

Olive-sided flycatcher

For about an hour during mid-morning, one single common merganser and two pairs flew round and round over the lake, quacking. They do this periodically for some reason. I cannot see any purpose to it.

Junco

24th May 2005

A classic pink/orange/gold sunrise predicted a windless morning and I should have gone across the lake and fallen more firewood trees, but how could I bear to waste this pristine morning on work? My destination: North Pass Lake.

The first pleasant surprises were close to home in Cabin Meadow,

Savannah sparrow

where both a "contralto warbler" and a savannah sparrow were singing. *Chip awheeeee p'chuck*, says the sparrow.

It took me a very long time to identify this bird because the first field guide I had stated it has no spot on its speckled breast, but these local birds often do. Later books accept the presence of chest spots.

Because of the recent cold, the snow patches were firm enough to hold me up and despite a fairly solid covering in places I made good progress to Loop Meadow. A nuthatch wheezed in the upper part of the forest—the first I have heard for some time as they left the feeder weeks ago. In Loop Meadow another savannah sparrow sang, accompanied by my favourite, a golden-crowned sparrow. *Me doh doh doh raaaaaaay* (the *ray* a warble). Heard only in the subalpine and higher, this call to me is the song of the land above the trees. It speaks of tundra and mountain-heather and heady mountain winds: an announcement that the world is where it should be.

Blooming mountain marsh marigolds and globe flowers were well represented at first after Loop Meadow, but soon the snow cover became complete. I wondered if I was going to be able to find any liquid water to drink for lunch, but a tiny trickle had melted a deep hole in the snow and I crouched down in it and listened to the sun-brilliant, windless silence. Probably 90 percent of the world's population have never heard silence like this.

I was not there all that long, but by the time I moved again, the snow surface had changed. The top had softened, and I boot-skated down for a while but soon began to crash through. From then on I sought the waterlogged, open spaces—icy on the toes but I could make better progress. Hiking boots are destined for a soggy existence at this time of year in my part of the world.

Shortly before Loop Meadow, some large footprints crossed a patch of snow along my path. A bear! On the radiophone last weekend Rosemary said the Precipice was crawling with bears. I could not determine if these tracks were from a black bear or a grizzly. They were large but melted out, and the claw marks were visible but close to the toes. So a black bear was most probable. Tracks mutate so quickly under these conditions I estimated they were probably made no earlier than yesterday morning. The animal had gone through the crust in places— either he/she had left it too late to travel on top or he/she was a great deal heavier than me.

Edith Meadow was full of mountain marsh marigolds, a constellation of clean new blossoms bordered by the sparkling creek with its clear, gravelly bottom (which the dogs kept muddying by flopping into it).

And best of all, no bugs. The early flush of mosquitoes on May 4th seems to have disappeared. That situation will not last too long, I fear.

25th May 2005

Another gorgeous day—but this time I could no longer put off the firewood chore. The lake was glass calm. A just past full moon hung over Flat Top Mountain, and all the brilliant white peaks around the lake kept arranging and rearranging themselves over their clones as I paddled along. It seemed sacrilege to shatter that perfection with a chainsaw.

Now that the snow had gone from the land I was able to fall trees a little farther back from the shore. The first one I chose seemed to be a cinch. It had an obvious lean toward a gap, the colour of the sawdust on the back cut was good, the wedge was clean and solid. I had angled the cuts right and there were no excessively heavy branches to swing the tree off course. But the darn thing shifted just enough to get royally hung up in its neighbour. I tried cutting a chunk off the bottom, but the tree twisted and jammed the saw. Fortunately, by using a long pole I had cut off with the axe, I was able to lever the trunk sufficiently to extract the saw. But apart from the bottom rounds, the tree would be lost to me unless it eventually fell over of its own accord.

That was doubly frustrating, because it was beautiful wood and almost all the other trees I tried had varying degrees of red rot. This is certainly not uncommon around the lake, but I have never seen such a concentration of it before. This was obviously why the pine beetle had zeroed in on this patch.

By early afternoon I'd had enough. I had cut up half a dozen trees and a couple of long-fallen snags. With the other trees I'd felled, plus a couple I would have to cut away from the trail around The Block, these would give me perhaps half a year's supply of firewood. Now all that remained was to split it, get it to the waterfront, load it into the canoe, paddle it home, unload it on the wharf and carry it up the steep path to the woodshed by hand. With luck, I will not have to do this work myself. There is an admirable organization called WWOOF: Willing Workers On Organic Farms. It gives people the opportunity to travel almost anywhere in the world and work for their keep. I have hosted wwoofers for a number of years now and found them to be lots of fun as well as a real boon as far as the heavy grunt work is concerned. So far, seven wwoofers are slated to come to Nuk Tessli this summer. When I go outside to stock up on supplies for the tourism business, which I will have to do before long, the first wwoofer will fly home with me.

Blackpoll warbler

By logging these trees now, I will have work on hand for her when she arrives.

As I canoed around the lake to the logging site, another new migrant made its presence known—a blackpoll warbler. When I first came here, I thought this bird's calls belonged to juncos, but the trill is much higher and shriller, and now I find it easy to tell them apart. One sang near the cabin and another on the west end of Crescent Island. From the logging site I could look across the lake to the eagles' nest, and through the binoculars I could still see the white head of a sitting bird. I first saw it sitting on April 27th. They apparently incubate for thirty-eight or forty days, so if anything is going to happen it should be any time now.

Two days of sun, and the leaf buds everywhere have made great strides. The bracted honeysuckle is always early and the huckleberries are freckled with green points. The Sitka mountain ash leaves are half out, and the slide alders are showing the tips of their meticulously creased leaves, which emerge sharply folded like a paper fan. Their catkins are just beginning to elongate. It is the only species of alder whose leaves and catkins open at the same time. The lance-fruited draba in my rock garden has been blooming for several days, and the Payson's draba is a mass of yellow buds just about to pop. Even the lovely villous cinquefoil has three open flowers on it.

It was such a warm, peaceful afternoon that I left the door open, but the windows were soon battered by large, black buzzing flies. Mosquitoes and blackflies are also beginning to be a nuisance, so reluctantly I retrieved the screen door from its winter home under the sleeping bench in Cabin Two and tacked screening over the windows that open. I went to bed with both the door and window wide open.

26th May 2005

Slept in this morning! It's hard to get enough sleep now the days are getting so long. It was sunrise when I woke—probably around 5:00 a.m. right now, but radio reception dies with the daylight so I can only guess.

No frost this morning and plus 20°C in the afternoon. Ants are everywhere all of a sudden, and I found a drowned, stubby-looking cricket, a species I've encountered half a dozen times before. They never make any cricket-like or cicada-like noises. They seem to be flightless, and they have very short, dumpy bodies and exaggerated hind legs. They live in holes in the ground, and this one must have got flooded out.

Tortoiseshell butterfly

I wrote sitting on the deck for a while. Two tortoiseshell and one mourning cloak butterfly flew by in that jerky, seemingly erratic way that butterflies have, but if you have ever tried to catch them you know what a good defence that flight pattern is. There were distant cackles from the flickers, a peep from a sandpiper and faint boomings from a grouse. A lone merganser cruised around and around for about half an hour, making its little grunty quacks. A hummingbird buzzed the feeder—the first female of the year. Then, while I sat and worked, a woodpecker peeped shrilly and inspected the bark of a tree for food. I haven't seen much of them for a while, although there has been quite a lot of drumming these last few days. Then I heard a dreaded window thump from the other side of the cabin. Running around, I found a second woodpecker, fortunately not badly hurt. And to my utter amazement, the the patch on the top of its head was not red, but yellow.

These birds were three-toed woodpeckers. I have identified this species only once before, but as it is so similar to the hairy unless seen at close range, it is likely that I have often missed it.

Then I heard another summer sound—a light aircraft! In my early years at Nuk Tessli I used to hear ski planes on any fine weekend throughout the winter, but apart from the planes that flew me in and out, and Floyd's mail drop, this is the first one of the year. It was Tweedsmuir Air's Beaver, heading toward the mountains, no doubt taking people on a flight-seeing tour. Which means that Stewart's Lodge at Nimpo Lake is up and running again. Now it is really starting to feel like summer.

27th May 2005
Record-breaking temperatures in the Lower Mainland—it was 33°C in Chilliwack—and it was 24°C here in the late afternoon. I don't know what it would have been at the hottest time of the day, as I was finally up once more on the North Ridge.

Three-toed woodpecker

A considerable amount of snow has disappeared during the last three days, but after Wiggly Creek (a savannah sparrow and a blackpoll warbler) there was more snow than bare ground, and it had the consistency of soft sugar. I floundered for a while (an olive-sided flycatcher; very close and its *Whup three beers* had a hiccup in the third note—it must have imbibed too much), then put on the snowshoes. I had chosen this style of footwear rather than skis as I can't walk very far in my three-pin ski boots (I keep tripping over the toes), so if I had packed the skis instead of the snowshoes, I would have had to bring the extra boots. A dog could have carried the spare pair—packing is, after all, what I keep them for—but sometimes it is more hassle to keep an eye on a dog than to carry stuff myself.

Perversely, as soon as I strapped on the snowshoes, I found a lot of exposed rocks. It was too much bother to put the snowshoes on and take them off every few steps, so I simply shuffled over the boulders with them. At least the bugs had been left behind—they had been quite a nuisance coming up the Steep Bit through the trees.

It was no longer easy to climb up the rockslide so I fumbled along the summer trail and used Long Meadow to gain altitude (two golden-crowned sparrows singing in different places, and a fox sparrow). Most of the meadow was snowbound except for a couple of big swaths in the middle where the snow had been melted by runoff. How clean and brilliant and sparkling was this water, flashing blue where it reflected the sky against the pure white snow.

Jacob's ladder

Payson's draba

Lance-fruited draba

White mountain-heather

Then the plateau—not a single stick of vegetation in sight here, but near the very last bush two silent robins hopped about over the snow. Insects are not only visible on this great expanse of white, they also become sluggish with the cold so they are easy pickings. All the thrushes take advantage of this largesse at both the beginning and the end of summer. The snow had drifted here and was deep and rotten—very hard work, even with the snowshoes. But behind this unbroken blanket, the Mammaries, exposed all winter to sun and wind, were barenaked.

So once on the saddle overlooking the North Pass, I strapped the snowshoes onto my backpack and had the pleasure of walking up dry, bare stones. This is where I had collected my draba and cinquefoil plants, and I was amazed to find them in exactly the same stage of development as they are in my rock garden 650 metres lower down. The mountain-heather was showing white buds and two Jacob's ladder plants had opened their delicate mauve blossoms.

At the top of the South Nipple, several gorgeous butter-yellow cushions of the villous cinquefoil were boldly displayed. They are stunning against the black-lichen-covered rocks. They were attended assiduously by a large brown bee. North American plants that grow away from habitation have not acquired attractive folk names, and the common name "villous cinquefoil" is derived from the Latin *Potentilla villosa*. "Villous" simply means "hairy," but for me the word always paints a picture of some

Villous cinquefoil

sleazy bearded gangster with a patch over his eye, a complete contrast to the open sunniness of these gorgeous flowers.

From these bumps along the North Ridge I can view my backyard. My lake was dark and somewhat drab in this blinding world of white. But higher ones were still frozen.

Ptarmigan tracks poked around a tiny piece of exposed mountain-heather surrounded by snow, but I did not see their maker. Living birdlife at this altitude was represented by half a dozen American pipits scattered among the stones. They are common every summer in the alpine here. They are slim birds, and they sit on rocks and bob up and down, waggling their long tails. They emit a high, thin little whistle. Sometimes I see horned larks as well, although they never seem to hang about for long and some years they are absent.

30th May 2005

Bizarre! Not only were we graced with the first strong display of northern lights for the year, but it was accompanied by thunder and lightning! Conditions that support one of these phenomena usually preclude the other. The aurora was visible through gaps in the thunderclouds—a very strong yellowish light covered the whole northern half of the sky, and columns of emerging and disappearing searchlights wavered over Halfway Mountain. Then, if that was not enough, while the aurora danced and the lightning flickered, a half moon rose over Louise O'Murphy's shoulder.

I have a coffee-table-sized garden in which I grow a few salad greens, snuggled between rocks along the trail to the lake. In it, when I went

Western toad

to fetch water today, was a half-grown western toad. It crept into the shade of some nearby willow bushes, but these toads often squat on baking hot sand or clay in full afternoon sunshine. One would not think an amphibian would revel in such conditions.

I phoned the Precipice to let them know I was still alive—the whole country down there is drowning in water and the mosquitoes are the worst that anyone can remember. While the radiophone was working I also managed to get through to Tweedsmuir Air and was informed that a plane will be free to pick me up on the 6th June. I had thought I might be ready for some company after a good part of five months in here alone, but I have no desire at all to go outside.

1st June 2005

Rain! Started yesterday in a dribbly sort of way. Fresh pollen has started to accumulate on the lake. It will be three weeks before the conifers bloom here, so I can only assume that this pollen must have floated up from lower elevations. Fir, cedar, aspen, cottonwood and spruce must all be flowering in the coastal valleys.

On still days the pollen forms a powdery skin on the water, and if we get a lot of hot, windless weather, it can accumulate in some sheltered bays as thick as cream. It becomes encrusted on the rocks by the shore, and as the water drops, it leaves a pollen tidemark like scum on a bathtub. Eventually, several layers of these tidemarks are created. They look like striations in the rock.

The rain is not heavy. Even after forty-eight hours, the ground within the dripline of the trees is still dry. It is quite cool and a little windy. Only 8°C today. The leaf development has halted.

The first yellow anemones are out in Cabin, Dandelion and Salamander meadows.

3rd June 2005

Calm and patchily sunny; canoed and hiked to Boundary Lake. The conditions were very similar to those on my last trip—the mountains poking above a strong mass of cloud, and a mix of light and shadows moving over the points of land, all faithfully reflected in the water. But when I was two-thirds of the way up Cohen Lake, a powder blue streak suddenly slashed across the far end. It made a gorgeous colour statement, but it came racing toward me, and the minute it struck I was plunged into wind-fighting mode.

There were still a few patches of snow along the trail, but I was little inconvenienced by them. Masses of pink swamp laurels sprawled everywhere, and lots of globe flowers, yellow mountain-heather, three or four marsh violets and two small sedges were blooming.

Birds were the usual—a robin, two kinglets, a mountain chickadee, two hermit thrushes and a "contralto warbler." A large number of sandpipers picked around the mudflats, which were now fully exposed. I could recognize three spotted sandpipers who foraged together; it is so disobliging of the others to look and sound so closely alike. Two loons swam on Cohen Lake and one on mine, and an eagle sat solidly on the nest. That makes thirty-seven days that they have been sitting. Are we going to have a big event soon?

The wind rose during the day, and coming home was pretty wild—it was just a question of steering the canoe and hanging on for a roller-coaster ride.

Yellow anemones

4th June 2005

No more joyriding—just the last cleanup and packing before I go out. Raked up the chips around the woodpile and picked up after the dogs.

While splitting wood, I noticed a woodpecker disappear into a hole in a dead tree where hairy woodpeckers nested about six years ago. The hole was hidden from me, and when I went around to look, I could see fresh excavations around the lip. Young woodpeckers are most entertaining. They hang out of the hole and *peep* violently; they have to be the noisiest offspring in the bird world. With luck, my time away will encourage the adults to settle in.

6th June 2005

Hail and heavy rain yesterday, and snow today! Three degrees centigrade at daylight and the ceiling about forty metres above the lake. If it doesn't get any worse, there is still just room for a plane to come in over the low ridge that defines the north end of my lake. The ground is white,

Marsh violets and yellow mountain-heather

the paper-thin covering on the roof is sliding inexorably down, hanging off the eaves in impossibly lacy sheets until it flops onto the deck in soft thumps.

As I was putting the shutters up, a male and two female mergansers did their flying around in circles and quacking thing; shortly afterward, a female returned alone, still quacking.

The pilot will be the first human being I have seen since the 2nd March (not counting the man who brought my mail—I didn't actually see him, only his plane). When I come home it will all be different. The place will be full of people.

SUMMER

17th June 2005

I arrived back yesterday morning in a Cessna 185 accompanied by Anneke, a tall, strong, thirty-year-old psychologist from Germany. She is the first of the seven wwoofers I am expecting this year.

It was rainy and cool during the ten days I was away and there has been snow at higher elevations. The foliage on the deciduous plants has moved only a little, but the variable willows by the wharf are spangled with globes of rich old-gold blossoms and I see flower buds on the black huckleberry bushes, even though their leaves are not yet properly out. It is the only edible berry that occurs in sufficient quantity and size to pick, and I watch the progress of its pinkish hanging urn-shaped blooms with more than passing interest. The country around Nuk Tessli is either sodden bog or dry rocky ridges, to which the centuries have added the scant duffy soil that supports the pine forest. In these areas the black huckleberry is probably the most common understorey plant. The little bells need insects to crawl into them before they are fertilized—which insects, apart from occasional ants of various sizes that I have observed doing their duty, I do not know. The best berry years have always had hot, sunny spells at huckleberry-flowering time; but whether the heat activates the insect, or stimulates the plant to release nectar and thus attract the insect, again I do not know. One year we had an absolutely stupendous crop that coincided with an unprecedented rash of yellowjackets during blossom time. I rarely see these insects here, and then only in the late summer, so this flush of spring wasps was as unusual as the succeeding crop of fruit.

The fox sparrow (just the one) is still singing heartily close to the cabin, plus a blackpoll warbler, a hermit thrush, a junco and a savannah sparrow. All seems quiet on the woodpecker front. A lone female merganser flew around and around, quacking—has she been doing this all the time that I have been gone?

19th June 2005

The bugs have hatched with a vengeance. They are never so bad around the cabins but it is very gloomy, humid and excruciatingly buggy in the bush. I must admit the cool, damp weather we are having does not bother me as much as it might, for at this time last year we had endless dry lightning storms and were gearing up for our terrible fire season. So as each crummy day unfolds, all I can think is that it is one fire-day less to worry about. The lack of wind exacerbated the bug problem, but it meant that Anneke and I could easily canoe across to the logging area and, if the calm held, bring back a load of wood.

I set my willing wwoofer to work with wedge and maul (and bug net) to split the bigger rounds of the first group of trees I had fallen onto the ice. They were too awkward to load in and out of the canoe if left whole. I took myself across to the other side of Big Inlet, as I wanted to tie flagging tape along a route that would eventually become a trail. At one time a horse trail went through there, and some parts of it would still be usable, but the original trapper never cleared it out well because his horses could wade through brush that would be uncomfortable for a hiker; on top of that, the trail had not been maintained for over thirty years and in many places there was no sign of it at all. The other nine-tenths of the lake already has a trail around it, and it is high time I finished the job.

No white head was visible above the eagles' nest as we paddled within binocular distance. Was a hatchling crouched in the bottom? The one they reared last year was not noticed until it was big enough to raise its head above the rim of the nest at the end of July.

20th June 2005

The longest day!

I went across the lake early and alone to beat any wind that might come up later, and brought back a full load of wood. Still no eagles.

It was dull and terribly buggy again; it is during these exact conditions at this time of year that I see black swifts. There are usually half a dozen and each flies in erratic circles, around and around, but all stay in a wide, loose group that gradually passes from west to east.

Are they visible because they fly lower in dull, cool weather? Or do they travel through only at that time? Insects fly lower as the barometer

Black swifts

drops—one has only to observe swallows to notice that. During high-pressure weather, swallows might be mere specks in the sky; when the barometer bottoms out, they practically skim the surface of the lake.

But the swifts might be visible under these conditions for a different reason. Although they look similar, swifts are not closely related to swallows on the evolutionary scale. Their nearest neighbours are nightjars. Some species of nightjar have the curious ability to go into a true hibernation state (except they do so in summer, in southern deserts, to escape the heat, and it is therefore called aestivation). Black swifts have a similar ability. They nest on rock ledges beside steep, shady creeks. In the cool dampness, the young are able to sink into a torpor so that they can be left alone for several days. The adults can then seek kinder climes during storms. Are the birds I see merely returning from a trip away?

Dandelion Meadow was looking very lush when we canoed past it,

Dandelion

and the patch near the head of the inlet was spangled with the golden flowers that have given it its name. They are a quarter of the size of those that appear in everyone's lawn but are still the same introduced species. Up here that makes them an anomaly: apart from a few edible nibbles that I try to grow in my tiny garden, which would not survive without my care, they are the only alien plant in this area. Everything else that grows or swims or walks or flies is just as nature made it, and that is pretty special in the world we have created for ourselves.

Native species of dandelion occur on scattered alpine ridges; these are distinguished from the alien weed by the green parts under the flower heads, which are not called sepals in composite flowers, but are known as involucre bracts or (in later books) as phyllaries. All dandelions have more than one ring of involucre bracts. On the native species they point up (and some of them have distinctive shapes); on the introduced weed the outer layer curls down.

26th June 2005

Nearly a week since I last wrote. It is very difficult to keep up with journals when I am active all day and there are people in my cabin almost every waking moment. I now have two more wwoofers and we all had a hard day yesterday so I told everyone they could sleep in, which they were only too pleased to do, but the suggestion was not altogether altruistic as it gives me an hour or two to catch up with myself.

On the 21st, I took the two women (Anneke now joined by Gabi from Australia) up to the North Ridge. (Klaus, the other wwoofer, is not a hiker: he prefers to get in a boat and fish.)

Rain was forecast but we had a spectacular sunny day with the panorama of mountain peaks clear all around. There were enough snow patches to make the alpine sparkle, but they did not inhibit our progress. A big bonus was the absence of bugs above the trees. The bare ground was absolutely running with water, and every creek and rill was smothered with starry fields of mountain marsh marigold and globe flowers. The two little tarns near the saddle that looks over North Pass (and that had been completely invisible on earlier trips) were still mostly frozen but with gorgeous greens, turquoises and blues of ice at various depths, and squiggles of open water in which the mountains were reflected.

The two women hiked much faster than I could, so they branched off to climb the highest point of the ridge, Avalanche Lake Lookout, leaving me to putter up the Mammaries. They are my favourite destination in summer in any case, as they have a much better display

Mountain marsh marigolds

South Nipple alpines

of alpine plants. The species I found up there were Jacob's ladder, fully out everywhere; roseroot—it has red flowers here; the sky-blue clusters of the tiny alpine forget-me-not; tight yellow cushions of Payson's draba (which is also still blooming in my garden—the lance-fruited draba is pretty much finished in both places) and also the barely noticeable, tiny white ashy draba; Ross' sandwort; western saxifrage a little lower down and the tufted saxifrage on the North Nipple; splendid golden displays of the villainous villous cinquefoil on the black-lichened bluffs; all five species of mountain-heather—red, yellow, pink and two white; bog-laurel in abundance—it is a good year for it; and even a few early paintbrushes and lupins.

There were also quite a few eight-petal avens on the west slope of the South Nipple. Elisabeth Beaubien from the University of Edmonton is studying this and a number of other plants, tying in their blooming times with the climate change. In Britain it has been observed that many species are opening three weeks earlier than they did twenty-five years ago. The plants chosen for Elisabeth's project include garden flowers like lilac, but there are a couple of alpines on the list. Dandelions, lodgepole pines, Labrador tea and bunchberries are other plants for which I can provide information. Some of the eight-petalled avens were all but finished and some in bud, so I figured they were more or less in the middle of their blooming period. They were fairly scattered—it has been too dry for too long and they are not doing well this year.

A winter wren was performing near Edith Meadow as we passed

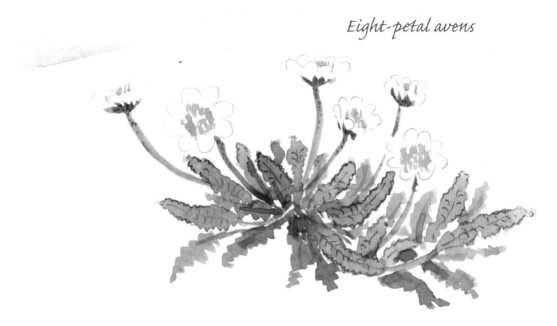

Eight-petal avens

through. At least I assume that's what it was. I have identified wrens here visually when they are not singing but have never quite been able to confirm that these pretty little cascades belongs to the same body, as they are most elusive at this time of year. I saw only three American pipits in the alpine. One I got a good look at: stripey throat and shoulder, drab underneath and a white flash on either side of the tail when it flew.

Anneke tells me that on the longest day in Germany they traditionally celebrate the solstice with a big bonfire. Last year's awful conflagration was started by a lightning strike on the 21st June, so a fire is the last thing I want to use to commemorate that!

Another trip to the alpine on the 23rd, but in a different direction. All of us headed across the lake and up the trail toward Fish Lake, the start of a route that eventually ends up at the nearest road. Klaus hiked up with us, but he was going to stop at Octopus Lake and see if he could catch some supper. For some reason the rainbow trout in this higher, very shallow lake are twice the size of those in my lake. Some years ago, when a lake survey was done throughout the area, it was discovered that this was a common pattern—the higher the lake, the bigger the fish. The only reason that the biologists could offer was the observation that the lower fish had a great many more parasites. No one can fly into Octopus Lake as it is too shallow; its bounty is reserved for the very few people who get there on foot.

The trail to the road was the first one I built, and after fifteen years, some of it was in sore need of attention. I started the women brushing a rather dense patch of subalpine fir that ran along the river just past the Octopus Lake bridge. After an hour or so, I left them to it and continued to the alpine. Some clients are hiking in by themselves in a week or so and I wanted to check on the cairns at the trail's upper end. A lot of the trail from the road is unmarked alpine, and most of it will stay that way, but without a few strategic cairns it is difficult to find the top of the trail where it enters the bush to descend to my lake. Last summer, three wwoofers helped build cairns across some of the open ground; I needed to make sure they were still standing, and to build more if there were spots that might be unclear.

I love that moment when you push through the last of the vegetation and the tundra unfolds. There is something so free about shrugging off the confines of the forest, even though I could not imagine living without its shelter or the useful materials it supplies. That day I had another bonus—a cold wind that kept the bugs away. I felt a bit guilty, as I knew the others would be half-blinded by bug nets, and bitten and sweaty and itchy all over.

Both bird and plant life were disappointing, however—a robin, a fox sparrow with an interesting variation to its song, a single golden-crowned sparrow, and a few pipits. Flowering plants were struggling in the cold.

On the 25th, leaving Klaus behind to tackle some carpentry work, the two women and I canoed up the lakes. Anneke and Gabi were to brush out the lower section of a trail I have just started that goes from the head of Cohen Lake to Flat Top Mountain. A valley up there hosts the most wonderful array of rock-alpines, some quite rare. One of these is the slender gentian; rarely sighted outside Mount Logan on the Alaska border. I have consequently called the place Gentian Valley.

slender gentian

Once again I had commandeered an old horse trail for a short stretch, but my route soon veers away from it and crosses a river. The rocks that can be used as stepping stones for most of the summer were hidden beneath spring runoff, so I thrashed through thick bushes upstream to gain access to a couple of fallen trees that precariously spanned the water. I slipped when almost across and would have fallen between them had my backpack not held me up.

A couple of cairns were needed immediately across the river, but there were no rocks handy and I had to trudge back and forth over a sodden bog to where a few stones poked out of a ridge. At one point there was a flutter of a bird from beneath my feet—no distinguishing marks that I could see. I did not want to disturb the bird unduly, but a quick look revealed the nest fifteen centimetres from my boots. It was on a patch of vegetation fractionally higher than the rest of the bog and half-hidden by short overhanging sedges. That was the material the bird had used for building, and inside the tidy grass ring were five blue-grey eggs liberally splotched with brown. I could feel the warmth rising from them as I carefully parted the vegetation to see them.

The river was very pretty and the sun was shining gloriously, but the bugs were horrendous. I have never known a year as bad. Blackflies as well as mosquitoes. The blackflies can get through my head net and they bat about my face and crawl behind my glasses. Sometimes it feels as though there are more inside than out and I take the head net off to let them go. They wouldn't seem as bad if I were walking, of course: bending down and slowly moving through dense brush exacerbates the condition.

I once read a magazine article that described a test for bug density. Expose a hand (with no bug dope on it) for five seconds, then slap it with the other. Even when the bugs are a nuisance, you may have nothing there. On that day my highest number was 13. The Canadian record is in the James Bay area, where it is something really gross like 150! But they get all their bugs in two weeks and then they are gone; Nuk Tessli will have varying degrees and species of biting flies for three and a half months.

27th June 2005

Another cool, rainy day. I made a quick trip to Salamander Meadow; I forgot my bug net so made an even quicker return.

And I found northern anemones; nagoonberries (they flower profusely but never make fruit); lots of marsh violets and yellow anemones; one or two pond-lily flowers (it's a poor year for them); bogbean blooming in Shady Pond; and the red, leatherleaf saxifrage's seed heads already beginning to show. Butterworts were out also—it is early for them. They are an insect-eating plant, one of four insectivorous species I have found in the area. They are sometimes known as bog violets because of the colour and shape of their blossoms, but they are not closely related. Butterworts do not gobble the bug with their flowers, as one visitor surmised, but trap tiny insects on their sticky leaves. The leaves are a pale neon green colour and feel slimy; this is due not only to the digestive enzyme that coats the surface, but also to small structures like the fleshy "teeth" on a fishing bird's tongue.

Other insect-eating plants in the area include two species of sundew, the long-leaved and the round-leaved which also digest passively with their leaves, and a floating common bladderwort that lives unattached to any soil and harvests its microscopic food with tiny bladders scattered along its feathery underwater stems; these can close in a fraction of a second. It is the stuff of horror stories—a free-swimming vegetable that actively gobbles its prey! Fortunately (for us) its victims are microscopic. Its yellow flower is commonly seen in the Chilcotin, but it must be close

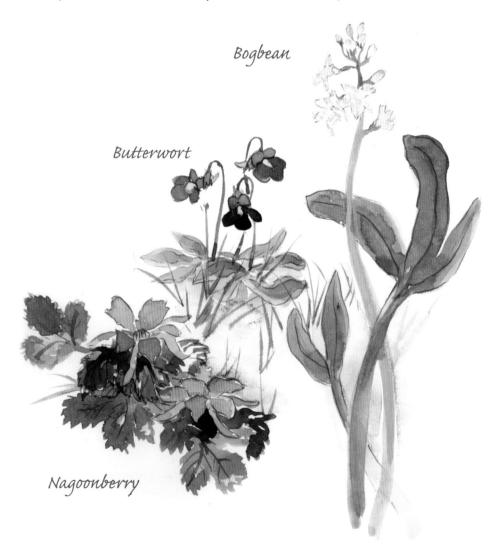

Bogbean

Butterwort

Nagoonberry

to the edge of its climatic range because it never blooms here.

The reason Nuk Tessli is so well endowed with these interesting plants is the acidity of the bogs. Acidity makes nitrogen unavailable to plants so they must acquire their dinner by other means.

The pride of the plants in Salamander Meadow is, however, the white bog-orchid. Sometimes known as bog candles, these twenty-five-centimetre flower stalks often grow among small sedges that make a mat as compact as a suburban lawn, so the orchids are very visible. In their prime, particularly when the sun shines, they let loose a wonderful freesia-like scent. Why, I don't know, as their main method of reproduction, as with most orchids, is vegetative and I rarely see insects interested in the blossoms.

Bog candles or white bog-orchid

28th June 2005

The women are away to Wilderness Lake on an overnight hike, Klaus went fishing and I canoed up the lakes to continue my trail-blazing work to Flat Top Mountain. I missed the photo op of the year just before reaching the portage. The male eagle was perched in full sun on a tree beside the river. As I glided past, a perfectly positioned half moon swam behind. But I was carrying a heavy load of trail tools as well as a coat and a lunch so had not brought the camera with me.

The next section of trail work involved tying flagging tape to branches and rocks to mark a new stretch. I ate lunch beside a small, peaty creek, thigh-deep but less than a pace across, on the far side of which grew a mixed clump of bog-laurel and marsh violets. The pink and mauve made a stunning colour combination.

On several occasions as I travelled through the open edges of the forest, juncos *dic-dic-dic*'ed madly, and I assume eggs have hatched. I have noticed that during incubation birds are exceedingly quiet, but as soon as the young pop out of the egg the warning cries come thick and fast. I believe this is not to scare off the intruder—rather, it alerts a predator that food is around. Instead, I believe the sounds are used to educate the babies. They are being told that what they are looking at means danger (even if they don't have their eyes open yet).

Back at home, the female hummingbird is starting to make regular visits to the feeder. The males almost never come now. When I lived in Cabin Two, I had a good place for the feeder right close to the window and could soon recognize individual female birds by their throat marks. But Cabin Three is in a windier spot, and the only place suitable to hang the sugar water is outside the porch where I cannot see it as well. All I am aware of is the hum and the dark silhouette as the birds dodge in and out to feed. It is still worth doing; many of my clients have never seen hummingbirds before so they are of great interest to them.

There seems to be no activity at the woodpecker hole, but I have seen the three-toed woodpeckers on quite a few occasions. Today both were cackling and investigating the loose bark on the slabs that encase the outhouse.

5th July 2005

The first two paying guests arrived a few days ago. Juliana was content to sit and enjoy while I took Emma up to The Lookout. The journey starts on the trail to the North Ridge, then branches off after the Steep Bit and runs along the edge of a rockslide before climbing up the far end of the bluffs. It takes only an hour or two to climb up there, but the view is well worth it.

The stretch along the bottom of the rockslide is quite pretty. At first the boulders are interspersed with mountain azaleas (their creamy trumpets were not quite open on this day).

A little farther along is a small meadow that laps against the rockslide like a green pool. The contrast between the great mass of tumbled, bare boulders and lawn-like sedges is abrupt. Pikas are common here. These guinea-pig-sized animals have the edge on "cute." They do not hibernate, but harvest plants and carry them to drying areas, often under an overhanging rock, then store them in their labyrinthine homes beneath the boulders for the winter.

It is difficult to spot the animals (particularly when the dogs are along) but their nasal warning peeps are commonplace. They also converse with a collection of high notes that reminded me of a kestrel's call when I first heard it. In fact it was quite a while before I realized that the sound was not made by a bird. This particular meadow must have been a pika home for many years, for little tracks are worn into the bog.

White mountain azalea

Pika

Past the meadow, one encounters a truly enormous tree (at least, for this area). It is a whitebark pine, perhaps twenty metres tall and well over a metre across at the butt. A third of the way up, it branches into two large, twisted limbs, which in turn branch and twist again. This tree is long dead, devoid of bark and weathered to a beautiful silvery grey. Around its base is a humongous squirrel midden. These underground cone caches must be used for hundreds of years; no doubt this one was started while the tree was still living. Twice since I have been at Nuk Tessli, the midden has been dug over by grizzlies, who toss the boulders willy-nilly. They are probably not after the squirrels so much as the oil-rich pine nuts that the whitebark pine produces. Every fall, bear droppings are full of the nut cases.

Because the tree is so weathered, I suspect it was killed by fire rather than disease. Disease-killed trees rot comparatively quickly, but fire-killed snags last centuries in this country. When I first came here I assumed the forest surrounding the cabins was short because of the altitude, but scattered remnants of giant trees have shown me that the climate can host a much taller forest, and I have come to the conclusion that what I am looking at today is the result of a big fire one or two hundred years ago. Scorched trunks and piles of charcoal still remain. Bluffs like the one below The Lookout act like chimneys; other large carcasses among the boulders show that the fire that last passed through here must have burned the rockface to the bone.

And so to the end of the bluff, and a scramble up some boulders. At once a nice panorama of the western mountains appears. At the top we pick our way among the rocks with their stunted trees and burned, weathered skeletons, back to the highest point. In the east, the two Otter lakes are backed by the distant blue Chilcotin plateau. To the south spreads my lake—the cabins are difficult to see unless the light shines in the right way on their brown metal roofs, but the islands surrounding the point are obvious enough. Behind is Louise O'Murphy—much distorted from this angle—and slightly to the right is a plethora of snowy peaks, mostly without names, dominated in the middle distance by the sharp wedge of Wilderness Mountain. Farther right is Flat Top Mountain, which drops off into The Trench. Behind that are the big guys, Monarch and Migma and a host of others marking the spine of the Coast Range.

After The Lookout, the trail follows a sparsely forested ridge to Loop Meadow. Lightning-struck trees are common along here, and not far past The Lookout is a tree that was blasted a couple of years after I came into the country. It had been a smallish whitebark, still living, and it had exploded. When it was first struck, shattered bits of pale, raw wood could be spotted for thirty metres in all directions. Now all are weathered and, except for the bigger parts of the trunk (which was split vertically into three chunks), are not so obvious. Twisted lines of duff and even freshly split rocks showed how the current had run along the roots and exploded there, too.

Round the base of what remains of the tree is now a vigorous forest of young lodgepole pines. About the time I left the tree-planting profession, experiments to add fertilizer to the planted tree were being conducted. Discussing this with a bunch of foresters on one occasion, I told them facetiously that I knew how to fertilize a forest—just get it struck by lightning. One of the foresters replied that in fact lightning does fix nitrogen into the soil. The young trees are certainly the most vigorous of all the young pines in the neighbourhood. It is interesting that they are lodgepole, which is not the same species as the parent tree.

The plane that came to fetch the two paying guests brought Mark Hobson and Paulette Laurendeau and Mark's parents. Mark is an artist who lives in Tofino. He and his family were self-catering, so I had only Gabi (Anneke had also gone), the two hikers who had come in on their own (and who had found my cairns with no trouble at all) plus myself to feed for the next few days.

Mark is very much the naturalist, and it was he who reported the first installment of what was to turn into a considerable drama. The woodpecker hole that I had assumed to be abandoned was in fact tenanted—not by woodpeckers but by flickers. They were not visible from my cabin, and as they had made no noise at all, I had not been aware of them. Mark observed quite the brouhaha. A squirrel stuck his head right into the hole, ignoring the parent flickers who were absolutely hammering him. Down flew everywhere; the squirrel escaped; and the parent birds disappeared. Surely no babies could have survived an onslaught like that.

But the following morning as I passed near the nest en route to the outhouse, an adult bird flew swiftly away. And out of the hole poked the heads of two large babies. They were pretty much adult sized but fuzzy. They occasionally made a soft, wheezy whine.

8th July 2005

It was Mark who spotted the three-toed woodpecker's nest as well, right at the edge of Corner Island. I had been hearing vague peepings coming and going on the wind for a day or two but had not yet isolated the source.

Baby flickers

Today I made time to go to the shore past the rockpile to check it out. Over a period of about fifteen minutes, an adult arrived seven times. The young were behaving just like the hairy woodpeckers had done when they occupied what is now the flicker's hole. An absolutely constant peeping without a single break. The only time they shut up was when the parent stuffed their mouths with food.

The weather has been wild, wild, wild. Mostly dull and rainy as well, so today's sun was welcome, but there was no respite from the wind and the lake was a deep blue slashed with vivid whitecaps. There is fresh snow on the mountains.

It won't be long before many of the birds quit singing and devote their energies to rearing their young, but this morning, now that the

Paintbrush and
Labrador tea

hikers have left, I was able to take time to listen. The ruby-crowned kinglet is still serenading from behind the outhouse, and today I noticed a pair of them giving agitated clicks around the dogs so assume they are educating babies. An olive-sided flycatcher (*Whup three beers*) has moved to within earshot of the cabin. I hear these birds repeatedly in the same three or four locations year after year. The fox sparrow still sings but less heartily; the yellow-rumped warbler is rarely heard, but the blackpoll warbler trills lustily (although never very early in the day). Hermit thrushes are late arrivals in the season and usually the last to quit performing. While hauling wood I heard a *Wheeeep?* which I always associate with young hermit thrushes so there must be some hatching going on there, too. Everything is happening at once.

I made a quick bug-swatting walk to Salamander Meadow. There was a bit of sun and the bog-orchids were splendid and drowning the world in scent. The butterworts were almost done (I dropped a few squashed bugs onto their leaves). The dandelions were pretty much over, too, although blossoms will appear all through the summer. Nearby, a nice clump of white Labrador tea and red paintbrush were blooming together.

12th July 2005

The Hobsons have left and a group of four women has arrived. As they are in the same cabin, which has a good view of the flicker hole, they were ideally placed to observe the next installment of the squirrel/flicker drama.

The squirrel got into the hole again and there was a big fight, ending with both squirrel and a bird tumbling out onto the ground, a drop of about eight metres. The guests rushed over; the squirrel ran away, leaving the injured fledgling alive but comatose. The bird had several oozing puncture wounds on its head. I did not expect it to survive but we put it in a closed cardboard box in a warm, quiet place, and it continued to breathe.

But the flicker was dead in the morning, and I was able to get a good look at it. The feet are four-toed, but the inner back digit is quite small. The colour under the wings was quite a surprise—it was a vivid yellow. I've only seen red-shafted flickers before and, wondering if this was simply a junior phase, I looked them up and found that the yellow-shafted and red-shafted flicker are considered one species, the northern flicker, but tend to occupy different areas. Yellow-shafted flickers occur in the east, but where they overlap there are hybrids. It is interesting to note that, same species or not, each wing colour goes with its own distinctive face mark. This fully grown youngster had the black moustache sported by the yellow-shafted strain.

This is what I think happened. The adults (whom I'd heard cackling off in the trees quite a bit before the incident) had been calling their youngsters from the nest. One flew, but the other did not quite feel ready so he was left undefended when the squirrel came back—encouraged, no doubt, by the absence of the adults as well as the youngster's demanding cries. This kind of thing must happen a lot. Flickers apparently lay six or eight eggs, so they must have a low breeding success rate.

I haven't heard the flickers for three days. Have they flown already, or has the squirrel been active over there, too?

18th July 2005

Early this morning I saw a fledgling perched on a branch, begging for food. It had a dumpy, spotty body and thick baby lips. The adult was invisible but a few song notes told me it was a fox sparrow. The fledgling was making little wheezes. At the same time the tree swallows have become very noisy. There seem to be six; no doubt some are hatchlings. They had a hard time flying in yesterday's wind.

I took a new client around The Block today. I was explaining to her that I had named Salamander Meadow because I occasionally saw these creatures in or around the pond by which we were standing. "Oh," she said casually, pointing to the ground beside her feet. "Here's one."

It must have metamorphosed recently, as it was quite small—full-grown adults are as long as a finger. And this creature's eyes really bulged out of the sides of its head. Its skin was vibrantly shiny black. The vivid yellow dorsal strip runs right from nose to tail tip (these are the northern, long-toed salamanders: the stripe is greener on the western species).

The sighting of an adult is quite unusual. Sometimes one can glimpse what looks like a yellow worm wriggling through the water as

Long-toed salamander

Larva

they dart toward shelter—only the yellow stripe stands out when they are swimming. I first became aware that salamanders existed here by spotting what seemed to be a tadpole with four legs in a subalpine pool. Later I saw several adult-sized larvae in another similar pond. They were brown all over and had feathery gills on the sides of their heads.

19th July 2005

Today I took the client up to the North Ridge. Cabin Meadow is full of the northern starwort, and at the higher elevations of the forest we ran into several blooming pygmy lewisia plants. It is a common species here but hard to find when not in flower, as the small, oddly succulent leaves become brown and withered and too well camouflaged to spot. The flower has a number of petals and is often somewhat lopsided—a characteristic of many species of the purslane family, most of which are easy to identify because they have the unusual number of two sepals.

Immediately above the Steep Bit, a trail crosses a small rill. The water bounces over rocks and spray keeps the shady banks damp, creating a tiny specialized ecosystem. In it (and in many other similar locations, above and below the treeline) grows a very odd-looking flower. Its blossoms are greenish and tiny, so are easily overlooked, but through a magnifying

Pygmy lewisia

glass the structures that are the petals are quite extraordinary. They look more like TV antennae than any part of a plant.

Only one species of mitrewort grows in this area, but others occur at lower elevations and most of them display these strangely shaded petals. Flower colour and pattern are designed exclusively to attract pollinators. What creature could be turned on by this peculiar display is hard to imagine. But it must work—every year little pockets, shaped like an upside-down bishop's mitre, are full of round, shiny black seeds.

Mitrewort

Blue grouse and chicks

On Long Meadow we encountered a blue grouse with three young just able to fly.

Oddly, the adult stayed absolutely motionless with none of the broken-wing demonstrations that are usual for that group of birds. I have often wondered about the effectiveness of that distraction, for several of my dogs have quickly learned that it means food and they ignore the adult and immediately hunt for the chicks. Presumably wild dogs do that, too.

Back home a family of yellow-rumped warblers were all over the place and the tree swallows were busy feeding their begging young—I counted seven birds altogether.

Young tree swallows

A fledged Clark's nutcracker demanded attention from its parents. The youngster was indistinguishable from the adults in appearance, but its call seemed a little softer compared with that of the two birds that were answering.

20th July 2005

To Boundary Lake. Windless and gloomy, and the bugs were a nightmare.

The bonus of the day was a wonderful patch of lupins scattered among waist-high nodding columbines. In this area, only the red columbine occurs. I always think the blossoms look like little helicopters whizzing about. Usually the blooming times of the lupins and the columbines do not synchronize very well, so this year's display was a treat.

24th July 2005

This morning the temperature was down to 2°C; it was quite misty at sunrise and the mountains floated like ethereal pink ghosts above the vapour. And it's a morning off! For about two hours. But soon I must clean the cabins and outhouses and do a couple of other chores before the next party, six women from the Lower Mainland, arrive early this afternoon.

A female rufous hummingbird, which has been feeding two or three times daily for the last three weeks, has stepped up her visiting. They always do that just before they leave. Very occasionally two birds fight over the feeder. At Nimpo and down in the Precipice, dozens of the little creatures whizz about the sugar water, and people tell me they refill the feeders twice a day. Here, were it not for the need to change the mix to keep it fresh, I would probably not fill the feeder more than twice a season.

The swallows appear to have flown. (Can't think why—there's still *plenty* of food for them.)

26th July 2005

The fox sparrow is still singing occasionally near the cabin. This is very late—usually they quit in the middle of the month. Later I saw a single adult looking for food. They have a marvellous way of scratching through the debris on the ground. Their legs kick so high and fast that vegetation is flung forty centimetres behind them. Which is a pretty impressive achievement for a bird only twelve centimetres long.

The hummingbird is still a frequent feeder—or maybe there is more than one, but if so they are never together. I am told they breed higher

Lupins and columbines

up in the krummholz. I've only once seen a young one here; it was already fledged and its wings quivered as it begged for food.

Young juncos are all over the place right now. They are spotted, although they already have the distinguishing white tail feathers. They make the most piercing feed-me call. It seems to penetrate my brain; the parents must either be very deaf or get frantic responding to it.

Clark's nutcrackers are frequenting the area around the cabins again. No doubt they are teaching their young where the best food can be found. The whitebark pine cones are not quite ripe, but I see a few birds testing them. Like many other creatures (including me), they are very fond of the oil-rich pine nuts that these cones contain.

A mature whitebark pine has a different silhouette from that of most northern conifers, being multibranched with a spreading crown, like an oak tree. As with most apparent aberrations in nature, there must be a reason for it.

The small nuts have no wings, so they cannot fly on the wind like the seeds of most conifers. The cones don't open naturally and if the seeds stay in them, they will become

Fledgling junco

rancid and rot. If they are taken too far under the ground, they cannot germinate. Once ripe, they do not stay viable for long. Consequently any seed that the squirrel stashes underground, even if it is not ingested, will not produce a tree. It is the Clark's nutcracker that ensures the whitebark's survival.

He can pack between thirty and sixty thousand (it depends which book you read) of the nuts to areas of open ground—often where a fire has burned—and there he buries two or three together just below the surface. The nutcracker never eats all that he gathers, and the remaining seeds

Clark's nutcracker and whitebark pine cones

grow into the new forest. Clumping can often be observed, although I believe that is more prevalent in the alpine areas, where most of the studies have been done. The nutcracker eats many kinds of food and the bird is widespread throughout a number of environments. But the whitebark pine would be doomed without the bird.

This is a classic example of how a plant and a bird have evolved together.

27th July 2005

To the Mammaries with the group from Vancouver today. Cool and buggy to the treeline but so cold above we were once more shivering, but blessedly spared the attentions of the flies.

Very little snow was visible in the alpine, although there was a big enough patch so that we could have a snowball fight in the lee of the saddle that looks over the North Pass. (A friend and her ten-year-old daughter had come with us, giving us a good excuse to play.)

This is normally the week when the flowers in the meadows below the Mammaries are at their best. And indeed, everything was there— red paintbrush, blue lupin, both the few-flowered and sword-leaved groundsel, yellow arnica, white valerian and the buttercup-like varied-leaved cinquefoil—but they were not as tall or as dense as they are in a good year. They have suffered through five years of summer drought and low winter snowfalls, so have drawn in their horns.

Two species of paintbrush grow in these meadows. The most vivid and abundant is the common red paintbrush, but the magenta few-flowered paintbrush is well represented, too.

The colour in these species is not the actual flower. Like poinsettias and flowering dogwoods, various plant structures like bracts or coloured leaves provide the signposts for the pollinator, and the flowers themselves are inconspicuous. The paintbrush flowers are green, pointy horns. They are actually tubes made of five petals, although two are so small as to be barely noticeable.

This means their pollinator must have a long tongue. The red colour is a magnet for hummingbirds. I've occasionally watched them feeding in the alpine, swooping from one green horn to the next in a graceful ballet very different from the mechanical in-out, in-out they perform at an artificial feeder. On one occasion of rare absolute stillness above the treeline, I observed a hummingbird hawkmoth performing the same function. It was the same size as the bird after which it is named and looked remarkably similar in its shape and movements. But its buzz was softer, like a cat's purr.

Inky gentian

*Two species of
paintbrush*

The paintbrush genus fascinates me. Although a number of species can be found from the Arctic to Mexico, it does not exist outside this continent. It can't easily be introduced anywhere else, as it has a little-understood semi-parasitic relationship with other plants. Some lower-elevation species grow among grass, and a certain amount of success has been achieved by sowing their seed with lawn clippings. But there are not many grasses in my backyard—it is too wet—so I do not know which plants these species need for survival.

Away from the bogs, the red mountain-heather was still splendid in places where the snow had lain late, and in a patch of peaty tundra, the remarkable inky gentians were blooming.

There are four species of gentian in the area, and none of them open wide like the better-known European species frequently grown in gardens. All the local native species are tiny. This one (except for a few albino populations) has blossoms of the most peculiar dark greenish blue colour. Presumably, since the flowers remain almost closed, they must be pollinated by insects. And presumably, because the colour is so odd, the pollinator must be very specific to the plant.

Two robins *dic dicced* frantically at the top of Long Meadow, so they must have had young.

We encountered a single willow ptarmigan in one place and later three adults with two half-grown young. All these adults displayed frantic "broken wings" to the dogs.

31st July 2005

It's getting light. The radio says it is 5:00 a.m. It is amazing how the days are shortening. The solstice occurred well over a month ago. Already the sunrise point—on the rare occasions when it is visible—has moved quite a way south.

A chip of waning moon is already high in a clear part of the sky, but clouds are racing and the wind is blowing. There was quite a heavy rain last night. The big mountains are hidden and there are more squalls and rain in the offing.

The six ladies and my friends left two days ago, and another friend, Sandy, arrived. Today a party of five will be flying to the Nimpo Lake Resort's cabin at Wilderness Lake, and Sandy and I will hike up there to meet them. It should take us four or five hours. I was hoping to tow extra canoes across the lake, to be ready for our return in three days time. But already the water is rough and Sandy is not a strong paddler, so I am not sure that we will be able to take more than one boat.

No fox sparrow has sung for the last couple of days. Nor has the blackpoll warbler for some time. The hermit thrush still makes an odd squawk at first light and I have seen it occasionally hunting for goodies. Their size and colouring is very similar to that of the fox sparrow, but they are slimmer and have a more upright stance, and they don't do the can-can when scratching for food.

6th August 2005

Home again after a wonderful trip and at last I have a chance to catch up on my journal.

By the time Sandy and I reached the trailhead on the 31st July it was raining pretty steadily. The weather was so socked in I wondered if the clients would be able to fly in. The trail first climbs up the established route to Fish Lake and veers off a short distance before Octopus Lake. The country just there is comparatively flat and pockmarked with hundreds of depressions, some merely bogs, others pothole sized, still others the size of house lots, and a few that one would class as lakes. Many of these holes are kettle ponds—depressions created by lumps of ice melting under the gravel once a glacier has retreated. Having no means of replenishing their water throughout the summer, they rapidly dry up, even though they may be full to the brim at high water. The trail runs beside one kettle pond that is as long as a football field (but skinnier and slightly curved). When I was working on the trail a couple of years ago, I stopped beside it for lunch one day. The pond was half empty, and my feet carried me across boulder-speckled mud, dried into polygon cracks, that was littered with

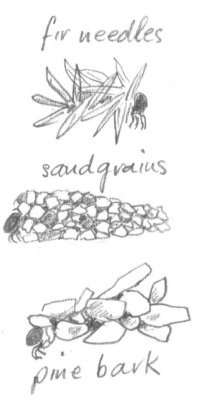

fir needles

sand grains

pine bark

Caddisfly larvae cases

empty caddisfly larvae cases. These animals are the hermit crabs of fresh water, except they make their own houses from debris at the bottom of ponds and creeks. Some choose coarse grains of sand, others use short fir needles or sticks. My books tell me that the insects stick them together with some kind of secretion—but where does the secretion come from? And how do they select the right-sized components? How do they place it on the tube? Why don't they themselves stick to it? And how do they attach themselves to it when they are dragging these houses along?

Each sand grain or bit of vegetable matter that the tube is constructed from seems to be about the same size. (The creatures usually favour one building material or the other, but I have occasionally found tubes made of a mixture.) The rocks around here are mostly granite derivatives, and as they break up they release chips of mica; many of the tiny glittering plates end up on these larval homes. I've often wondered if the larvae that live in gold-bearing creeks end up packing around gold-plated houses.

The resistance of these shelters to the substances over which the larva crawls to find organic particles of food must be tremendous. If you see a faint, convoluted trail in otherwise featureless silt at the bottom of a pond, it has probably been made by one of these larvae. But I've also seen them living in roaring rivers, clinging to vegetation in a current that would knock me off my feet. They must be immensely strong, not only to prevent themselves from being washed away but also to stop the tube from being torn off them.

What was the meaning of these thousands of discarded houses in the dried mud of this kettle pond? Had the larvae all pupated? The two-centimetre-long, floppy-winged adults are not all that common. Besides, they live for several years in the larval stage. What do they do when the pond dries up? Do they survive by burrowing into the silt? Can they take their homes with them if they do that? Or do they discard their houses and build new ones every time the water covers them and they reemerge? And if they have such a short growing season compared with those that live in year-round ponds, does that retard their development into adults?

And why were there so many in this particular pond, both in and out of the water on that day? On subsequent trips through there I've seen hardly any. In fact, they seem to have died out everywhere in the area. I like to show the cases to my guests (who get nature lectures whether they want them or not), but latterly I have had a really hard time finding any.

Caddisfly larvae were not the only occupants of that pond on the day I stopped for lunch. Looking into the water I was presented with a vibrant tableau worthy of any sci-fi architect trying to create a futuristic city in an environment not bound by the laws of gravity.

Public transport was represented by various-sized beetle larvae with their soft, elongated bodies and bulging eyes. Their multiple legs churned steadily but they travelled very slowly and tended to stay suspended between the surface of the water and the bottom, which was about thirty centimetres deep just there. The faster vehicles were the adult beetles. The taxis were as big as my little fingernail; each bore a white chevron on its back and two well-developed legs that served as underwater oars. The smaller private cars, which were zipping about everywhere, were the exact nut-brown colour of an unopened pussy willow bud. The tiny minis were a little more retiring—they were no bigger than radish seeds. But all were trundling urgently up and down in their weightless environment with an enviable disregard for gravity.

Water beetles

To further the analogy with a sci-fi village, all these creatures needed airborne oxygen to breathe. They periodically rose to the surface, stuck their bums through the meniscus and collected their oxygen packs in the form of a silvery bubble tucked under the ends of their wing covers (or pincers, in the case of the larvae) before resuming their busy lives.

After Kettle Pond Flat, the country begins to slope upward and the water is concentrated into a river that tumbles fast and furious on its rocky journey down the mountain. Sandy and I had been tramping for about two and a half hours at that point, and we crawled under the thick, spreading skirts of a short pine to stay out of the rain while we had a snack. The clouds broke a little but the rain did not quit, it merely pounded down in silver rods backlit by a watery gleam of light. But the weather must have been better lower down, for it was at this point that we heard the Beaver flying in with our guests. I had informed them that Sandy and I would not arrive until at least midday. They had been told where to find the key to the cabin.

Where the trees become denser, the trail leaves the water and climbs up open slopes of mountain-heather and bog to the foot of a rockslide before dropping down again toward Wilderness Lake. This last section is well endowed with flowers. That day the gloom and wet emphasized the colours so the blossoms glowed like jewels. Paintbrushes were ruby red, and the fragrant pillars of the white bog-orchids were the tallest and most dense I have ever seen. Their perfume filled the air.

Flowers in the rain were all very well, but we wanted to hike high into the alpine. Wilderness Lake is eight kilometres south of mine as the plane flies and less than two hundred metres higher in altitude. But tucked under Wilderness Mountain, the highest peak in the immediate area, the valley enjoys a much colder and stormier climate. Glaciers keep the waters frigid, and the shadow of the mountain's great wall prevents the sun from reaching the lake during much of the winter. The cabin is perched on a windswept knoll surrounded by the last straggles of krummholz, and the view up the lake is pure alpine.

The weather gods were kind to us and our clients, however, and the 1st August was gorgeous—cold but bright with fat clouds racing dark shadows over the land. Our destination was a moraine lake trapped behind a wall of gravel and boulders left by retreating ice. The biggest icefield in the immediate area runs behind it, tumbling into the water at one end, twisting itself tortuously around some rocks on its way. Lumps of ice often float about in the water; I've seen wolves up there more than once.

First we picked a route up the side of Wilderness Lake (no trail here) and then we had to cross a creek. Usually it is not a lot of trouble to boulder-hop to the other side, but it was running so high with all the rain that we had to hunt quite a bit to find a way over. Beyond that is Dry Lake. It is marked as a slab of water on the map but must have been very shallow when the aerial photo was taken forty years ago, for now the only water is a creek at the edge. The rest is covered with

Caribou

short willows and is flat as a board. Often I walk along it, but again the excessive precipitation made the creek just too much of a nuisance to cross and we hiked along the side. Three mountain caribou were grazing among the willows.

The caribou have a curious high-stepping, prancing gait. They bounce away—then come back and stare, then bounce, then return and stare again. They can go on like this for quite a while.

At the far end of Dry Lake, we crossed the valley and climbed to the moraine. The view is hidden until the top is reached, and then all the effort seems worth it. The gently sloping silt leads to greyish glacial

Mountain fireweed

flour-laden water backed by the contorted icefield. In the soft, barren soil alongside the lake were the tracks of a grizzly mother and her cub.

It is now possible to walk right up onto the glacier. When I first saw the place fifteen years ago (long before anyone had ever landed a plane there, let alone built a cabin), the glacier stretched much farther and there were ice caves along its snout. The colour inside the ice is amazing—various shades of greeny blue almost to black, the darker hues not unlike those of inky gentian blossoms. The roofs of the caves had been sculpted into hollows and points by the thawing, and water dripped and plonked musically.

The moraine wall is flattish on top and a mountain goat track runs along it, making it easy to walk up there. The side that faces the ice is sunny, but one can feel the blast of cold from the glacier even on a hot summer day. And yet it is amazing how many flowers manage to grab hold of the surface. A few gorgeous magenta mountain fireweeds and their smaller relative, the alpine willowherb; some straggly arnica (two species, mountain and alpine); several very robust cut-leaved fleabanes and some woody-stemmed alpine fleabanes; and in one spot a patch of elegant hawksbeard, *Crepis elegans*. This last looks somewhat like a tiny dark-stemmed, many-branched version of the sow thistle that grows as an introduced wayside weed in populated areas.

Cut-leaved fleabane

Mountain arnica

Dark or red leaves and stems are common in the alpine. As the same species has green leaves in shadier locations, I think the colour is either a reaction to or a defence against the ultraviolet bombardment that these plants are subjected to in the alpine. Another, more familiar defence against the climate that is often used by alpine plants is hairiness. In the botanical world hairiness does not keep the organism warm, as is popularly thought, but has evolved to prevent dehydration by cutting down wind speed against the plant's sensitive tissue.

A golden-crowned sparrow and a savannah sparrow had sung near the cabin when we left that morning, a semi-palmated sandpiper had

Rock ptarmigan

scurried along the little beach, and up on the moraine we ran into two species of ptarmigan, the willow and the rock. The latter is smaller and speaks with a whistle rather than the grating cackle of the former.

One rock ptarmigan was alone but the other two appeared to be a pair. I saw no young with them but they were all displaying to the dogs so they must have had babies somewhere.

The eastern slopes of the Coast Range are dry and cold, and their elevation gain on average is gentle. The western slopes are steep and rugged, and immediately much wetter. Once off the moraine we hiked to a viewpoint above a valley that plunged down through a V set with a perfect oval turquoise lake. In creeks, glacial flour is grey and slimy, but when it enters a lake it becomes suspended and refracts the light in such a way as to give off an amazing range of blues and greens. Mats of the finger-sized pink trumpets of Davidson's penstemon (illustrated on page 89) can be found by the viewpoint. When the penstemon is flowering, the pink and turquoise vibrate.

10th August 2005

Summer, all of a sudden, is just about done. The Labrador tea along the water-front is long finished, and the bunchberry has only a few flowers left. There has been no sign of either eagle beside the nest. I think their forty days and forty nights of sitting was for nought.

To the North Ridge yesterday with a different group of guests. From the North Nipple we cut straight down the face of the mountain. Ahead among the rocks and dense ground cover of kinnikinnick was a blob of yellow, which proved to be a magnificent clump of a groundsel relative.

This one is only hand high with silvery leaves and a clump of very rich cadmium yellow blossoms, giving the plant one of its common names: silvery butterweed although its more usual name is woolly groundsel.

Silvery Butterweed or Woolly Groundsel

An unusual visitor around the cabins right now is a great blue heron. Seen perhaps five times during my tenure here, this elegant, ungainly bird so familiar in a coastal landscape seems huge besides the short trees at this elevation.

Belted kingfishers

I heard the first belted kingfisher yesterday. The mechanical rattle of its call is a sound of waning summer, as that is the only time they visit. They dive into the water like arrows.

The hummingbirds seem to have gone.

11th August 2005

A gorgeous, dreamy, sunny day. At last it is actually hot. This time last year it was 30°C and cloudless, day after day after day. Or it would have been, had we not been smothered by smoke. Then I would have given anything for the weather we have had this year, but now it's the other way around. I guess we are never satisfied.

The busiest part of my tourist season is over. Sandy flew out with the last group and everyone remaining is off on their own hikes, leaving me to bake bread and cook. It is the first time I have had to myself for weeks but I can hardly enjoy it—whenever I sit down, I collapse.

The sun has brought the butterflies out. In the alpine, when I was up there the other day, clodius parnassians, alpines, checkerspots and a species of blue butterfly were flitting about.

Closer to home there are painted ladies and mourning cloaks, all newly hatched and fresh. Glittering dragonflies are patrolling up and down along the waterfront.

Alpine butterflies

Clodius parnassian

Ross' Alpine

blue

Painted Lady

Dragonfly

13th August 2005

The mosquitoes have all but finished, the blackflies should be but aren't, and the no-see-ums are gone (they never last more than three weeks). But with this sunny weather the horseflies are becoming a pest. You can't win. Some are black and tan with black eyes, and these are the true horseflies, apparently. The slightly smaller ones with green eyes or eyes striped green and grey, called greenheads, are much commoner in the alpine.

They are not supposed to bite humans or feast on blood, but the ones that live here obviously haven't read the book. Their mandibles are like blunt chisels and the insects use them with no attempt at finesse when they try to take a bite, unlike the sneaky blackflies, which at least have the grace to anaesthetize you first. No animal can tolerate the pain when horseflies attempt to penetrate—how do the insects ever manage to suck long enough to get a meal?

There are about a hundred small fish about the wharf right now. They come during high summer every year. They are not trout, but

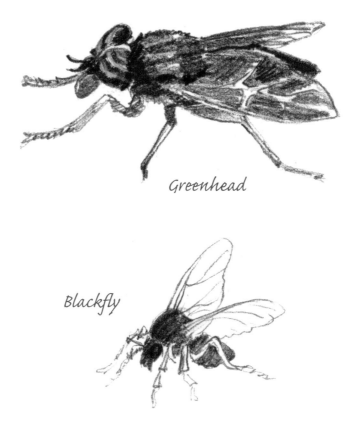

Greenhead

Blackfly

most likely squawfish. One year, I had an eight-year-old visitor who spent hours swatting horseflies and feeding them to the fish. She made a lot of piscine friends.

The current group of visitors canoed themselves around to Sunrise Viewpoint this morning and were rewarded with a beauty. It is worth the early start to paddle around behind Crescent Island, as the lake is often ruffled by a dawn wind but the water in the lagoon is dead calm and mirrors the pink and orange shapes of the mountains.

When the people came for breakfast, they commented on some "ducks" they had disturbed. The two adults had a slew of babies and all of a sudden the whole lot tore across the water like little powerboats. These would have been common mergansers—they have this rather marvellous ability to cover territory by flailing their wings like paddlewheels. Very handy when the young cannot yet fly. However, it can't save them from every danger—mergansers lay up to a dozen eggs, which means the species has a poor survival rate. Two brown adults means two females; often broods get mixed up and they all end

Merganser family

up following one mother, which is why you sometimes see them with twenty or more babies in tow.

14th August 2005
It has been a bit smoky these last few days, but the fires could be hundreds of kilometres away. It is just a blue haze, nothing like last year's smog. By afternoon a southwest breeze sprang up. I thought it would clear the smoke, but if anything it got worse and at sunset an orange half moon hung in the west.

A single adult merganser with eight half-grown young swam near the cabin. It could not have been the ones the other visitors observed, as the babies they saw were tiny. So it looks as though at least three pairs of adults bred successfully on either my lake or Cohen Lake.

The present visitors are due to fly out later today. Now I will have only a scattering of paying guests to deal with. But on this plane I am expecting the fall crop of wwoofers. There are four: a couple and a brother and sister, all German, although the two pairs have not met before.

18th August 2005
My new wwoofers are excellent! Point them in the right direction with trail-brushing tools in their hands and they go through the bush like a dose of salts. They have done some serious work on the Gentian Valley trail. It goes through a lot of wet meadows far from rock sources, but four pairs of strong legs have made light work of carrying stones to build the cairns. The weather has deteriorated again and the mosquitoes, which are usually no bother at this time of year, are just as bad as the blackflies and horseflies. So once more we view the world through a veil.

The male eagle has been flying overhead this last couple of days. The hummingbirds have definitely gone—the current guests, who live in the Okanagan, the wine-growing area of British Columbia, said theirs went on August 7th and it would have been the same here, give or take a day. Interesting that the hummingbirds should leave from such different regions at the same time. People say the birds are encouraged to stay longer than they should if feeders are left up, but I think their departure is stimulated by other triggers.

It was suddenly much cooler yesterday, and mist spiralled up from the water. There is a definite early fall feel to the air.

25th August 2005

Last night (or rather this morning—I was told later that it was 3:00 a.m.) I awoke to an extraordinarily light sky full of the most dazzling northern lights. I got everyone out of bed—the paying guests in the cabins and the wwoofers in the tents. Everything was happening— strobe lights whizzing at us seemingly from treetop level, white towers of flickering flames streaking up to a central point above our heads. Three-quarters of the sky was covered. They look as though you could touch them but they are about 160 kilometres high, much farther away than any clouds we ever see.

All of a sudden there are juncos everywhere—a flock of ten was feeding near the portage, where the wwoofers built a bridge across the river to complete the circuit of the lake trail, and I have heard juncos singing a couple of times near the cabin. I have noticed that as the birds get ready to move, they often make a bit of an attempt at their spring songs.

28th August 2005

The last two days have been wild and squally. This morning I woke in the dark to see stars in the gaps between the clouds. Orion now completely clears Louise O'Murphy before first light.

Having an hour to spare during the day, I made a quick trip to some of my best berry patches. But as expected after the cool rainy summer, the crop is a disaster. I'll take two wwoofers with me and see what we can find but I suspect that we will pick the whole lot in an afternoon, a job that would take me a week or ten days in a better year.

Black huckleberries

29th August 2005

Poured again last night but there seems to be a slight improvement today. There was a lurid orange sunrise, with slashed and disturbed clouds flying over the heavens and a bank of fog streaming in over the top of Louise O'Murphy like an express train. Fresh snow lies above the treeline on the mountains around the lake. A hermit thrush sang a bit this morning and a fox sparrow gave half his song once.

Mice have moved into the attic big time.

5th September 2005

A clear night with brilliant stars; now there is a lemon glow in the northeast presaging a cloudless sunrise. The wwoofers have gone, the paying guests have thinned out—the only person here other than me is a German man called Guenther. I will take him to the sunrise viewpoint this morning. It's his first chance to see a sunrise, as the weather has been lousy since he arrived. The clear sky this morning indicated a frost; I could feel the stiffness of the ground when I went to the outhouse in the dark. Sometimes the frosts start as early as the middle of August, but this is only the second this year.

The sunrise was a dream. The frost-slick canoe slid into the water as if greased. The reward—a classic Chinese painting of rising mists and floating peaks, all bathed in pink then orange then gold, and all faithfully reflected in the lagoon. Guenther lives in an apartment in Berlin. He grew up in the former East Germany and has not travelled much except in his mind; he told me he had never seen anything more beautiful in his life (he is seventy years old).

After breakfast I took Guenther to Boundary Lake. It was a gorgeous day, although a bit windy at the end. The sun is lower and the light is richer now. Not much yellow in the deciduous bushes yet, but on the bare upper slopes of the mountains the tundra is reddish brown. The lake, in the stiff breeze, was somewhere between cobalt and ultramarine. The mountains wore powdered wigs of new snow.

6th September 2005

Suddenly there are all kinds of birds again. They are heading to their winter grounds. Today I heard or saw the following:

two great horned owls, one calling about an octave and a half higher than the other;

a ruby-crowned kinglet (singing in its broken-record phase);

a fox sparrow singing briefly;

a robin;

two Clark's nutcrackers;

two loons;

a belted kingfisher (it is constantly around);

spruce grouse (they are suddenly quite common);

a small group of what I think are golden-crowned kinglets—I hear them every year at this time for a week or two;

a winter wren, not singing and not at all shy;

a raven;

two or three lbjs ("little brown jobs"—various species of small brown birds that are difficult to distinguish from each other).

9th September 2005

To The Lookout this afternoon. Four waxwings were swooping and fluttering over a patch of kinnikinnick at the bottom of the bluffs, no doubt after the berries. This plant bloomed profusely everywhere this year and its berry crop is the best ever. (The fruit is not very palatable for humans, unfortunately.)

Spectacular northern lights again last night. I woke Guenther and suggested he come to the wharf, the best place to observe them. The whole sky was full of flickering searchlights, wavering curtains and strobes. Guenther went to Nova Scotia a couple of years ago, so this is not his first trip to Canada, but he said: "I have seen so many things here I have never seen before."

12th September 2005

Two more visitors arrived. It was windless when they came, and the blackflies were horrible. The fall ones seem to be slightly smaller than the spring ones, so I assume they are different species. I will occasionally react to a bite in spring, but never in the fall; however, I absolutely hate the feel of their little feet on my skin. They gather on the windows, hundreds of them crawling up and falling and crawling up again, a constant movement, like one of those models constructed to demonstrate kinetic energy.

Yesterday I took the axe and blazed the new trail that the wwoofers made between the portage and Canoe Inlet. It had been marked with flagging tape up until now. It passes through the area I logged in the spring. When I whacked several of the trees to make the cut for the blaze, I realized that quite a large number were dead. Their needles were green, but the trunk had no resilience and when the bark was removed I could see the characteristic blue staining of the fungus carried by the pine beetle. Little piles of orange sawdust lay at the bases of the trees. So I can expect quite a big brown patch of forest there next year. I have noticed one or two other brown trees in the area—a couple at the river end of Cranberry Meadows and another one at the northeast end of the lake.

13th September 2005
To the Mammaries. A dull-bright day, and the blackflies a pest until we cleared Long Meadow. In the alpine, the plants wore their fall livery. A common species of rush had turned a deep, vibrant yellow, exactly the colour of the dead flicker baby's wing. The rush grew in tufts like painter's brushstrokes, but if one actually painted that on a landscape it would look corny. A late patch of harebells (round-leaved, not the more common alpine harebell) crouched under a bonsai'ed clump of subalpine fir.

Round-leaved harebell

Stonecrop

A few spreading stonecrops were out. The lance-leaved stonecrop has identical starry yellow flowers but blooms much earlier. On most of our walks the spreading stonecrop is represented only by its extraordinary globular succulent leaves, usually bright red in the alpine, so that they look like strings of berries.

It is not only humans that are fooled. When I put a plant in my rock garden, the birds pecked it to bits. Higher up, tiny red and yellow snow willows formed a brilliant scattering of gems among the black-lichened rocks. The roseroot's leaves have turned a soft purple-red.

I have never figured out why, but the top tarn below the saddle that overlooks the North Pass always remains full, even when the meadows are dry, but at the end of the season the lower pond is always nearly empty. Today they were like eyes (the lower one with a wide black rim as if outlined in kohl), as they reflected the blue-patched sky, the colour so perfectly complemented by the yellow-painted tundra that surrounded them.

14th September 2005

This afternoon saw a rash of birds. About a dozen yellow-rumped warblers came through (much drabber now) and then five robins, several unidentifiables much the same size, and a Steller's jay—minus his tail, which made him look very odd.

18th September 2005

Earlier, the lake was deep blue and slashed with whitecaps; now it is grey and ditto, and it is raining furiously. Gusts of rain smash into the window and cascade in wavering curtains down the glass.

Five friends from Australia are here at the moment. On the 16th we went to Boundary Lake. Nine mergansers swam on Cohen Lake (no doubt the same group I observed before; now they are all the same size) and also a pair of brown-speckled ducks with long necks and slim heads. Would they be northern pintails? We spotted another pair of these farther up the river. There were no sandpipers on the mudflats and only one or two juncos en route. Sometimes the mudflats are a storybook of tracks at this low-water time of year—moose, deer, goats, wolves—but all we saw that day were some not very fresh black bear prints.

Steller's Jay minus tail

Yesterday we went up the Mammaries. Being Australian (and one couple lives on the tropical north Queensland coast), my guests were anxious to see snow, but all I could offer them was a tiny remnant of the snow patch in the lee of the saddle looking over the North Pass. It has often snowed at cabin level by mid-September but of course the powers that be didn't oblige when snow was wanted. It was chilly enough, with some clouds, but we got a lot of sun as well. The bright light washed out fall colours on the tundra; in any case I think they are already past their best.

At the top of Long Meadow, when we were going up and coming down, was a group of pale grey, robin-sized birds that obviously weren't thrushes, but at first I could not figure them out. Some seemed to have a slight powder-blue cast as they made short flights between the bushes. They must have found goodies to eat, as they didn't seem to be in any hurry to move on. One surprised me immensely by doing a pretty good job of hovering like a kestrel.

At home, I confirmed that they were mountain bluebirds, observed here only once before, in the spring, when they wore their bright breeding plumage and looked quite different. The books tell me hovering is a characteristic of this species, also that they often collect in quite big flocks in the alpine in the fall.

Marmots and pikas were evident five days ago, when I was up there

Mountain bluebirds

with Guenther and two other clients, but on this trip we heard none. Have the marmots gone to bed already?

19th September 2005

I woke to moonshine on brilliant, thick new snow on Louise O'Murphy. It floated like a white cloud against the pale night sky. The moon itself was high over Anvil Mountain, sailing in and out of dark clouds edged with moonlight. The lake was a crumpled carpet of shining silver foil.

I am completely alone for the first time in three and a half months. Solitude is very important to my peace of mind; I must leave for the outside world again at the beginning of October to prepare for this fall's

Hoary marmot

book tour. Without these precious two weeks of solitude I would not be able to function out there.

20th September 2005

The equinox. A few snow flurries this morning but it didn't settle here. The wind seems to be dying down and a large patch of clear sky is moving over.

The Pacific willow on the waterfront hangs its long yellow leaves like bamboo brushstrokes on a Chinese painting. The round leaves of the variable willow are still green. Now is the time to harvest "willow roses." Dried, they make interesting house ornaments to give to friends. They are created by an insect that gets into the terminal leaf bud. Not all species of willow are affected, but each one that succumbs produces a different-shaped "rose."

Willow rose

During this last month, different clients have reported seeing a grizzly with cubs near Otter Lake.

This afternoon, Raffi kept growling and barking and looking very alert. Neither of my dogs makes much noise normally. I suspect the bears were within nose-shot.

21st September 2005

A clear night, the moon brilliant, and minus 3°C on the thermometer. The sun now has to climb over Louise O'Murphy's right buttock before it reaches the cabin. In two days I have lost more than half an hour of sunshine.

The haze started soon after sunrise and thickened during the afternoon, creating a raw damp. It grew darker and darker, and suddenly hailstones the size of peas pounded down. The ground was white in seconds. Frozen pellets roared on the metal roof and bounced off rocks like the balls in a lottery number dispenser. The hail lasted half an hour and then turned to thick, wet snow before petering out. The ice turned to slush quickly on the rocks but lingered on the ground between them, where it had accumulated to a depth of two centimetres.

The only living thing I saw all day was a junco.

22rd September 2005

Minus 4°C and diamond clear! The moon not quite half full so the stars were brilliant. The fairy fire of frost sparkles accompanied me to the outhouse on my first trip of the day. I sometimes curse at having to stick my nose out of doors on inclement mornings, but I miss that little window of nature when I am visiting the city, where, even if I walk the dogs before daylight, the city's unrelenting glow destroys the pleasure of the dark. As daylight came, the lake was a mirror, and when the sun touched the water, mist rose and gave a dreamy quality to the perfect day. This is fall as it should be.

A tidy-up firewood day was scheduled. Pieces of it were scattered about the lake, either because there had been no room in the canoe or, as happened on one occasion, several rounds were dumped overboard because it became too windy to get home safely with a full load. I had planned to travel fast in case the wind got up, but the jewelled calm was so bewitching I dawdled along the sunlit shore, loath to break the stillness. Two pairs of red-necked grebes and four gulls hung on the water.

Most of the firewood was on the shady side of the lake, where yesterday's ice fall still lay in a crunchy skin. I had thought that there were only a few rounds, but I ended up having a pretty good load. Fortunately, the day stayed calm. A straggling lump of clouds over the

Red-necked grebes

north end of the lake made bizarre shapes with their reflections.

Between the logging area and the cabins, four more birds sat on the water. They seemed to be pale-bodied ducks with brown heads. They were leery of me and although they did not fly away, they swam faster than I could paddle with my juggernaut of cargo. Through the binoculars I could make out startlingly blue beaks. At home, my books informed me that they were lesser scaup, which are "abundant, especially inland," but I have never seen them before.

23rd September 2005

Another clear, sparkling morning and I set off early for the North Pass, intending to cross it to the waterfall. The sun was low and the frost was white on Cabin Meadow, and the hoar-edged sedges glittered with all the colours of the rainbow.

The recent snow had melted from all sunny ground, but a surprising amount still lay in shady spots—despite yesterday's sunshine, the true

Lesser scaup

temperature must have stayed below freezing all day. A clump of droop-leaved fireweed, which had been such a pretty red a couple of days ago, was now wilted and brown.

I made good time to Loop Meadow, and then branched off onto the North Pass Trail. I hadn't been that way since the first mountain marsh marigold was blooming and the yellow-rumped warbler flashed his neon flags at me. Now the ponds and lakes were perfect mirrors to the brilliant white, newly whitewashed mountains and the deep blue sky. Just before the trail dips to North Pass Lake I came upon a vast dug-up area that had once held lupins, decorated with the fattest rounds of bear poop that I have ever seen. They were as thick as my wrist: that must have been one big bear. But they were frozen, and the dogs were only vaguely interested, so I knew the animal was not close.

Along the stony parts of the old horse trail (which has all but disappeared; I plan to improve it some day) around the North Pass Lake, the berry-leaved stonecrops were still blooming. I stopped as usual for a drink and lunch at Incompetence Creek where it pours out of Incompetence Valley (named by the outfitter's guide; he took a party of hunters along here; they saw twelve ptarmigan, shot off their guns and missed the lot). Behind me a shady bluff, on which grow five species

Flowers at the waterfall

of saxifrage in the summer, was greyed by its sprinkle of snow; with backlighting it was a perfect silvery foil to clumps of ground-hugging yellow-leaved arctic willow with their silky candles of puffy seeds. This sunny, windless spell has made all the fruits explode.

Then into the upper valley, where I disturbed nine willow ptarmigan already half white. The sky was beginning to haze over and a small wind rippled the two shallow lakes. I've often seen caribou here, but not today. The waterfall is at the upper end of the valley. It comes down from yet another lake in a series of pretty cascades. The best way to appreciate its various sections is to start at the bottom and scramble up the rocks beside it.

I was surprised to find a few ragged flowers still blooming near the base. It was quite shady, so last winter's snow must have lain late there and the spray would keep the frosts at bay. There were some magenta fireweed blossoms, snow-battered mauve fleabanes and yellow arnicas. A smaller relative of the fireweed thrust vertical red-brown pods up like a forest of fingers.

The glacier-smoothed rocks beside the next section are too scoured by ancient ice and rushing water to hold much in the way of plant life. The stream was still noisy and crashing despite its end-of-summer low. I

Dipper at waterfall

heard a grating cackle—familiar, but at first I did not place it because it was out of context—it was a sound I normally hear only in the winter. At the top of the cascade, peering down at me, was an American dipper.

Directly across the spray-white creek on a small ledge were a couple of waterlogged plants and a head-sized lump of brown moss that appeared to have a hole in one side. Could this possibly be the dipper's nest? It was spangled with water—I could see drops glinting right inside. It would surely be much wetter in the spring. Either the dippers incubate well or, like the swifts, the young have extra mechanisms for combatting the cold. Later, at home, *Birds of British Columbia* confirmed that the moss ball was indeed a dipper nest. The book has a picture of one perched right on the top of a pointed rock in the middle of a boulder-filled river.

When I first came to Nuk Tessli, a snowfield always blocked the end of the lake below the falls. In recent summers, the snow patch has disappeared by September. So I was very surprised to find one this year. It was big enough to make passage around the edge of the lake quite difficult. Where had it come from? Last summer's baking heat and fires would have melted it right away, and last winter's snowfall was pretty feeble. The cool, damp summer must have preserved almost all of it. This is very encouraging; perhaps other drastically shrunk snow patches have received a new lease on life. Permanent or at least late-lying snow is essential to the ecology of these mountains. Rain runs off right away, flooding lowlands; snow releases water all through the summer. It is one reason why clear-cut logging at high elevations is so ecologically disastrous. A forest will shade the snow beneath its branches and retain it for months longer than on a sun-blasted clear-cut. Foresters like the earlier bare ground of a clear-cut. They maintain that the growing season is longer and that the seedlings will establish themselves better. But the resulting early, violent runoff not only washes away the nutrients, it also erodes the very mountains themselves.

Instead of staying on the trail, I took a different route home. I cut down through the upper montane forest and followed the creek that runs down to Big Beach. I hadn't visited that spot since photographing the Barrow's goldeneyes in their pool before the ice went out. The creek runs through a dank, shady gully but is quite an interesting bit of topography. I will modify and brush out the game trail that runs up there next summer. That will make a nice loop hike going up Otter Creek to The Lookout, then down Big Beach Creek and back to the cabins along the shore of the lake.

25th September 2005

The local channel of the radiophone is busy at nights. People are checking in with each other from planes, pickups and cabins. Hunting season has started.

27th September 2005

A calm morning again after a couple of stormy days, so I took the chainsaw up the lake to cut out a tree that had fallen on the trail—but when I got there, I found I had forgotten to put gas in the saw! However, I had brought my camera along and I took several shots of "totem poles." These are fun, and they can only be done when the water is dead calm.

If you take pictures of rocks reflected in the water and then stand them on end, all sorts of interesting faces can be seen. I have a lot of fun with these in slide shows. Always there is someone who cannot figure them out until I flip the slide so that the rocks and their reflections lie as they do in nature. You have to be quick when photographing them. If you wait too long, the little ripples from the canoe reach the shore and destroy the mirror effect.

Reflections

This might well be the last good day. The satellite weather pictures on the computer show major disturbances: Puntzi is supposed to be cloudy, but Bella Coola is forecasting unremitting rain for the next five days.

It will also be my last day alone. The last clients of the season arrive tomorrow and when they leave, I will fly out with them.

28th September 2005

A wild, warm wind and a chip of a moon in an almost clear sky when I woke, but daylight brought a racing cloud cover, whitecaps and walls of rain. Now it is mid-afternoon, pouring rain and as dark as twilight. I guess we were in the Puntzi forecast district first thing, but we're in the Bella Coola one now. The clients haven't made it in yet. Louise O'Murphy and Cradle Mountain are both invisible—until they clear, no one will be able to fly.

30th September 2005

A pink tinge of afterglow in the east at sundown yesterday, and at night the cloud broke so that the stars were brilliant and huge, hanging like lamps. Just before first light, a fingernail paring of moon rose, lying on its back like a catcher's mitt with the old moon faintly reddish within its palm. There were some colourful clouds at sunrise but too many to let the light reach the big mountains; in any case they were mostly hidden within their own vaporous shrouds. The bits that are showing are palely plastered with wet-looking snow.

The clients sneaked in underneath a low ceiling late yesterday afternoon. They are self-catering and are off on a hike at the moment. They are foresters—no strangers to the bush—so they will be able to find their own way around.

I went around The Block for the first time in weeks. A lot of the leaves have gone, beaten to mush by the wind and rain. The huckleberry bushes are bare and the willows still harbour a few drooping yellow pennants, but along Otter Creek most of the leaves lay like slabs of yellow paint on the rocks or swirled through the dark water under the laced branches. A single translucent clump of red highbush cranberries hung in the bare branches like a little glowing lantern.

Slide alder leaves do not change colour when they wither; they either drop off while still green or simply shrivel and brown. Next year's catkins are already well developed, little fat sausage fingers sticking out from the ends of the twigs. The denuded sand-coloured mountain azalea twigs sport new lime-green buds.

There is a calm place along Otter Creek where the water horsetail grows. This fascinating group of plants are evolutionary remnants of the forests that eventually became coal. They have curious joints along their stems that can be pulled apart like Christmas crackers. Water horsetail has few side stems at this altitude (it doesn't actually possess leaves) and spends most of its life as a thin, green vertical stalk closely surrounded by others of its kind. Once the frost hits these plants, they droop over.

The tips of the hollow stems trail on the water, and the results, with their reflections, make the most wonderful calligraphy.

1st October 2005

Tomorrow is the day we all leave. The clients will go back to work and I will start a different kind of job: organizing my annual fall book tour. The clients had not arranged a departure time before they came in and I cannot get through on the radiophone, so I have no idea when tomorrow's plane will come.

It is chilly but calmer; bits of mountain keep emerging from the clouds.

2nd October 2005

Minus 5°C and the most spectacular sunrise of the year! The eastern sky was lurid and the mountains were blood red against a wall of pinker vapour. But before the colour had spread halfway down the mountains, it went out like a light and a thick ground-level fog rolled in from the east. No working phone and uncertain weather. There is nothing we can do but wait.

FALL

Since the early 1990s, I have spent most of October, November and a good part of December on the road promoting my books, artwork, and tourist business. Book tours are fun, exasperating, exhilarating and absolutely exhausting. They take a big chunk out of my life every fall. But without them I would fade into obscurity and my writing income would plummet and I would be lost. It is very gratifying to have a certain amount of fame, which I seem to have in the far west of Canada, but somehow the fortune that is said to go with it has never materialized. My business, the Nuk Tessli Alpine Experience, cannot pay all of my bills, and fall book tours have become a way of life.

During my first years here, however, I spent most of the fall and winter in the mountains. Those were the days before the internet—even before the radiophone. My only communication was with my dogs and with my journal. The dogs would be happy to make contributions if they could, but it is my journal from those early years that tells the story of fall at Nuk Tessli.

15th October 1988

The ravens that were around with the storms earlier this month have left again. I rarely see them except just before bad weather in the fall. Do these harbingers of doom need wild weather to survive?

Yesterday it rained for a while, gently, with a few flakes of snow mixed in. Then there was an extraordinarily beautiful moment when the clouds, which hung low enough to almost touch the water, began to dissolve from the top, and a wonderful bluish, pearly luminescence covered everything.

Raven

25th October 1990

I heard loons calling through the falling snow and I launched the canoe, as much to give the dogs a run as anything. It is strange to be on the lake while the flakes are tumbling from the sky. They whirl to the grey water to meet their darker reflections whirling up. The instant they connect, they vanish.

28th October 1990

Quite a pleasant day, and I launched the canoe again. The snow still lies in patches, but most of it has melted. The wind held off for quite a while and I ended up paddling right around the lake. The weather was very unsettled, though. Only bits of the big mountains are visible, and toward Nimpo the sky was as black as a bruise. The sun made an effort to shine onto my lake, but it was half-veiled by silently streaming snow clouds. Very calm on the water at first, but the wind got me in the end. It was so strong on the last stretch coming back past the inlets that I could not hold the nose of the canoe into it and ended up paddling backward. Some waterfowl had taken the opportunity to rest in the brief earlier calm on their journey south. Three Barrow's goldeneyes sat at one end of the lake. They were either all females or males that had

Long-tailed duck

donned their winter plumage, for their colour was a uniform brown. Four other ducks were at the opposite end of the lake. They had white faces, black eyes and thin, needle-like tails. The books tell me they are oldsquaws, a species now called the long-tailed duck. A pair of red-necked grebes swam close by.

The robins and varied thrushes were no longer about; the only migrant left was an occasional junco. A dipper bobbed by the water at the edge of Big Beach. And as I write, eight crows have just roosted briefly on the trees beyond my window. Crows are even less common than ravens at Nuk Tessli so that is quite a surprise.

31st October 1990

A family of trumpeter swans visited today, two white adults and four grey adolescents. They acknowledged my presence with a couple of warning honks but were content to glide in a circle and land behind Kojo's Island. They nest in Alaska but winter along the coastal inlets and on Vancouver Island. Their call, a soft *parp* like the honk of a toy truck, is one of those sounds that once heard can never be forgotten.

In the late afternoon I walked past the spot where I camped while I built the first cabin at Nuk Tessli. A tiny bay there gives a pretty view up the lake. The clear sun was hanging low over Mount Monarch, and its reflection slithered over the softly moving water, little golden worms wriggling back and forth. The tiny bay had iced over, which reflected the colour in quite a different way. "Camera!" I thought, but even as I watched, plop! The sun was gone.

5th November 1988

As I press my face against the window I see flakes falling swiftly against the night, glinting as they tumble within the realm lit by my candles.

Trumpeter swans

Everything is rapidly whitening. It is mild, so some of it will melt, but I think that this will be the start of the permanent ground cover. It is very quiet. The fire flutters faintly in the stove and one of the candles evinces a soft hissing. It must have a faulty wick.

6th November 1988
When daylight came, every window was falling, falling, and every reflective surface inside echoed the movement: a shiny pot, the egg flip, the edge of my glasses, the glass covering the paintings hanging on the walls. Wherever I looked, there was a silent tumbling and falling. By late morning the snow was over twenty centimetres deep. The landscape trembled with piled snow, softly balancing on every leaf and twig. Whitebark pine needles are arranged in roundish clumps, and each of these bore a perfect pyramid of snow like ice cream in a cone.

Along the lakeshore, the rocks poking out of the water were cushioned with caps of white; between them mats of grey sludge had formed. The colourscape had been transformed from browns and sooty greys to stark black and white with soft greys in between. Clark's nutcracker colours. I tried to launch the canoe into the lake, but the sludge was too thick and I could make no headway. Later the snow stopped and there was a very brief calm, but then the wind switched and became an instant gale. Within minutes, the sludge had broken up in the waves, and when the snow began again it was driving horizontally and slapping against the glass. Heavy lumps dislodged from the trees flopped against the windows as that delicate, breathless world was smashed.

12th November 1988
More gales. The wildest winds always barrel in from the west and northwest, and under these conditions the slate grey lake is slashed with

foam. I can see the gusts of wind coming, manifest by darker bands on the water, which come closer and closer until the wind hits the shore with a roar.

Too wild for the canoe, so I walked round to Sunrise Viewpoint, slithering on the snow-covered rocks. The thin ice that stopped me from canoeing in the shallow water behind Crescent Island a couple of weeks ago has consolidated to an opaque mat dotted with weak areas and spring holes. The two inlets are both frozen, too. The ice must have spread a bit farther before this wind—in storms like these it breaks apart. Plates as clear as window glass have been driven up onto the shore.

13th November 1990

Wild, wild wind—and rain. Bizarrely, radio signals sometimes come through clearly in the heavy rain, and I learned that the storm is devastating the Lower Mainland. It travelled up north, just touched my lake, turned around and went back again. The tree trunks are black with rain. Black, foam-slashed water heaves under a black, boiling sky. Water batters the windows and cascades down the glass.

Down south, road closures, floods, rockslides, mudslides and avalanches are occurring. In one instance, seventy souls had to be helicoptered to safety. Livestock are drowned—4,500 turkeys on one farm alone. Apparently it is only since 1987 that storms of this ferocity have become a regular thing. A combination of global warming and poor environmental practices, which may or may not amount to the same thing.

16th November 1988

When the storm abated, I launched the canoe for what would probably be the last paddle of the year. A couple of days of comparative calm and the mat of ice has crept farther up the lake again. I had to break the pieces that had formed between the islands to get into the open water. (I had drilled a hole into the end of the axe handle and passed a loop of string through it and around my wrist so that I would not lose it when I bent over the gunwale to hack at the ice.) I could not stay on the water long, as the wind became too unpleasant. The ice was tissue thin, and when the wind rose the ice undulated like a skin of oil before it cracked and broke. It hissed and grated and tinkled along the shore. During the night the big gusts started again, and I could hear the sibilance of the shattering ice over the wind's roar. By daylight much of the new ice had gone and snow was falling.

17th November 1988

Minus 12°C at first light, clear and calm. Mist is rising thickly from the remaining open water. New ice has formed far beyond the islands, and the frost ferns are thick on the porch windows.

I'd forgotten what sunshine could look like! How exquisite is the new snow on the trees; the greenish new ice on the lake; the golden mist backlit by the low, early sun; the rich blue of the open water beyond the islands; and the bright white mountains lying beyond.

I slithered through the snow around the north end of the lake again, taking the axe with me to check the ice behind Crescent Island. I could walk on it in places. Where I cut through to the water, it was ten centimetres thick. Five centimetres is supposed to be enough to support a person, but I shuffled along with great care as I never knew where it might be weak. The water is very shallow, especially at this time of year, but I have no means of knowing how deep the underlying sludge is. If I fell through, I might not have anything to stand on.

Last spring I read an article in *Discover* magazine about organisms that I never knew existed even though they were first discovered half a century ago. They live in the cold sludge at the bottom of deep seas, or closer to the surface in chilly climates near the poles. They are apparently so numerous that they are estimated to form 35 percent of the world's biomass, which is a pretty amazing figure if you think about it.

There are apparently two groups of organisms. The one closest to the earth's centre produces methane in such quantities that were it to be released unchecked it would erupt with such force that the world would be engulfed in major tsunamis. However, the upper group of organisms break down this methane into harmless gases. No one knows how these organisms can synthesize energy in such a cold, dark environment. One way that they conserve it is that they have such a slow metabolism that they may reproduce once in a thousand or even ten thousand years!

When my lake was surveyed by Fish and Wildlife, the measurable depth across the widest part was sixty metres, but the whole bottom appeared to be flat. Behind Crescent Island it is less than a metre deep during low water. But an organic sludge covers the bottom and I have not been able to reach anything solid below the surface with either pole or paddle.

The apparent flat bottom in the middle of the lake would indicate that the whole of it is carpeted with tons and tons of this sludge. It is a cold lake even at the surface, and it must be pretty chilly and dark at the bottom. Would these amazing organisms be living down there?

These microbes are anaerobic; that is, oxygen is poisonous to them.

A number of anaerobic organisms exist quite happily on the surface of the earth—the gangrene family of bacteria is one, and it includes the organism that causes the deadly food poisoning botulism. But some anaerobic microbes are very beneficial, notably those that fix nitrogen into the soil. Gangrene thrives only in unaerated wounds; botulism develops in improperly canned food. Nitrogen-fixing organisms maintain their anaerobic status by stimulating the plant to form nodules in which they can live away from the poisonous air.

Most westerners are schooled by two doctrines: one is that we have all evolved from single-celled animals, and the other is that life cannot exist without oxygen. But if 35 percent of our earth's biomass consists of single-celled organisms that can live on our earth without the benefit of oxygen, what is there to prevent a complicated life force developing on another planet where oxygen cannot exist?

18th November 1988
Sullen and dreary with a fitful wind and bursts of squally snow. Whitecaps slash the open water and the new ice is undulating up and down, up and down, long cracks showing with the movement. The edge is crumbling and being slowly pushed back toward the shore.

20th November 1990
Calm, minus 10°C, and the lake froze all over last night. The water must have been cold enough for a while but simply had to wait for the wind to drop. The ice is covered with frost flowers.

I had to chop through seven centimetres by the shore in order to get water. I had not intended to step onto it but slipped and crashed down on it anyway. The ice never so much as trembled.

10th December 1989
I took the axe and went for a walk on the lake. Snow had fallen intermittently, and even a thin layer will insulate the ice and slow down the freezing process. As far as I could make out, there were fifteen centimetres wherever I tested, but it was difficult to determine accurately because the covering of snow has created overflow, and as soon as I whacked the ice, water ran into the crack and hid where I was trying to chop. Beyond the ring of islands there were several spring holes. When I stood several metres away, the water in the holes jiggled, which made me feel very insecure even though logic told me there was nothing to fear.

Near the outlet I ran into some extensive overflow, my boots creating dark, water-filled prints in the snow. The sinking feeling that went along with it was disconcerting. The outlet pool was partially frozen and across it was the neatly stitched track of a fox.

16th December 1989

A day-long fog, which is unusual at Nuk Tessli. How often do I hear on the forecast "fog in low-lying areas" and know that Nimpo Lake and Charlotte Lake will be socked in while I am bathed in sunshine?

But this fog persisted. A barely noticeable air movement came from the east, and every surface facing it acquired a two-centimetre pelt of ice crystals. By afternoon the top of the fog sank to just above lake level and the mountains reared up like islands. Just before the end of day, the sun dropped into a gap below the lid of overcast and painted all the vapour and furry haloes of frost a brilliant gold. Within a breath, the fog was sucked up and gone.

17th December 1989

Today I walked to the north end of the lake, crossed behind Crescent Island and continued to the outlet again. There were quite a lot of tracks in the thin snow: fox, and what is probably a mink (a weasel of some sort, and about the right size for a mink), some ptarmigan and even a moose. He had used the footprints I had made the other day. Did he reason that because one heavy creature had walked there, the ice would be safe for him?

18th December 1990

Today it was minus 20°C but with a bite to it far below that of the thermometer reading. Mucus froze in my nose and my eyelashes stuck together when I blinked.

When it warmed up a little I put snowshoes on and trudged to the edge of Cabin Meadow to cut a crooked little subalpine fir that was jammed under a fallen log. It would never amount to anything as a forest tree. I shook the snow off and dragged it inside to thaw. Later I will decorate it with ornaments collected over the years and chains made out of flagging tape. Christmas is a time to think of friends, and I do so whether I

My Christmas tree

am with them or not. I never mind being at Nuk Tessli alone. In any case, the real point of these shenanigans as far as I am concerned is the winter solstice and the returning light. I celebrate that, wherever I am, with all my heart.

22nd December 1990

Dark is defeated! Sun is coming back! It showed its defiance by setting in a blaze of glory last night, all the more spectacular as cloud had obscured it all day. (Perversely, without the cloud, the sun could not have flung its vivid reds all over the sky.)

It was clear and 40 below this morning. My thermometer is not calibrated below minus 35°C, but the column of alcohol runs lower. I'm never sure how accurate these thermometers are, particularly at this altitude: wouldn't a thinner air affect the reading?

I saw two birds yesterday, the first moving creatures for a while. A Clark's nutcracker checked out the cabin—I won't have any fat for it until I next go out to stores, so it has to go hungry—and a trumpeter swan flew down to the lake near the outlet and sat on the ice for several hours. It is unusual to see them alone. They like ice to rest on; presumably they feel safe where they can see predators coming. They seem to be able tolerate extremely bitter conditions. Once I saw four of them sit in much the same place for two days in mist snow with a very nasty east wind in minus 28°C temperatures.

24th December 1989

The sun rose over Kojo's Island and splayed long-fingered shadows across the lake. It poured into the cabin and flooded the room with light. Soon the wind started. At first the snow slithered across the ice like snakes: the light never loses its orange cast for the couple of weeks around the shortest day, and it was like looking across an orange-gold river. As the wind strengthened, the snow was whipped into spinning clouds whirling and dancing down the lake, golden dervishes that danced to celebrate the sun's new life.

Clark's Nutcracker

APPENDIX 1

NUK TESSLI ALPINE AND SUBALPINE PLANTS

Means not positively identified.

Abies lasiocarpa – Subalpine Fir.
Achillea millefolium var. *alpicola* – Yarrow.
Aconitum delphiniifolium – Alpine Monkshood.
Actea rubra – Bane Berry.
Agoseris aurantiaca – Gold False Dandelion.
      A. glauca – Orange False Dandelion.
Alnus viridus ssp *spicata* – Slide Alder.
Amelanchier alnifolium – Saskatoon Berry.
Anaphalis margaritacea – Everlasting daisy.
Androsace septentrionalis – Fairy Candelabra.
Anemone multifida – Cut-leafed Anemone.
      A. parviflora – Northern Anemone.
      A. richardsonii – Yellow Anemone.
Angelica genuflecta – Angelica.
Antennaria alpina – Alpine Pussy Toes.
      A. lanata – Woolley Pussy Toes.
      A. mycrophylla – Pussy Toes.
      A. racemosa – Racemose Pussy Toes.
Aqueligia formosa – Western Columbine.
Arabis holboelli – Holboelli's Rock Cress.
      A. lyalli – Lyall's Rock Cress.
Arcenthobium americanum – Pine Mistletoe.
Arctostaphylos uva-ursi – Kinnikinnik.
Arenaria minuarta – Ross' Sandwort.
Arnica amplexicaulus.
      A. angustifolia – Alpine Arnica.
      A. cordifolia – Heart-leaved Arnica.
      A. latifolia – Mountain Arnica.
      A. mollis – Hairy Arnica.
      A. parryii – Parry's Arnica.
      A. frigida.
Artimesia norwegica – Mountain Mugwort.
Aster foliaceus – Leafy Aster.
      A. modestus – Great Northern Aster.
Betula glandulosa – Dwarf Birch.
Botrychium lunaria – Grape-leaved Moonwort.
      B. multifidium – Moonwort.
Callitriche sp.
Caltha leptosepala – Mountain Marsh Marigold.
Campanula lasiocarpa – Mountain Harebell.
      C. rotundifolia – Round-leaved Harebell.
Cardamine bellidifolia – Bittercress.
      C. oligosperma.
      C. pensylvatinica.
Cassiope mertensiana – White Mountain Heather.
      C. tetragona – Arctic Heather.

Castilleja miniata – Common Red Paintbrush.
> *C. parviflora* – Small-flowered Paintbrush.
> *C. rhexifolia.*
Cerastium alpinum – Alpine Chickweed.
> **C. berrigeanum.*
Chimophila umbellata var. *occidentalis* – Prince's Pine.
Collinsia rattanii – Blue-eyed Mary.
Cornus canadensis – Creeping Dogwood.
Crepis elegans – Elegant Hawksbeard.
> *C. nan* – Dwarf Hawksbeard.
Cryptogramma crispa.
Crystopteris fragiilis.
> *C. montana.*
Draba paysonii – Payson's Draba.
> **D. praealta.*
Drosera longifolia – Long-leaved Sundew.
> *D. rotundifolia* – Round-leaved Sundew.
Dryas drummondii (rare here, on gravelly morraine) – Mountain Avens.
> *D. octapetala* – Eight-petalled Avens.
Empetrium nigrum – Crowberry.
Epilobium anagalidifolium – Alpine Fireweed.
> *E. angustifolium* – Fireweed.
> *E. latifolium* – Mountain Fireweed.
> *E. luteum* – Yellow Fireweed.
> *E. palustre* – Marsh Fireweed.
Equisitum arvense – Common Horsetail.
> *E. fluviatile* – Water Horsetail.
> *E. hyemale* – Scouring Rush.
> *E. variegatum.*
Erigeron acris.
> *E. alpina* – Alpine Fleabane.
> *E. compositus* – Cut-leafed Fleabane.
> *E. humilis* – Woolley Fleabane.
> *E. perigrinus* var. *callianthemus* – Purple Mountain Daisy.
Eriophorum polystachion – Cotton Grass.
Gallium trifidum.
> **G. triflorum* – Small-flowered Goose Grass.
Gaultheria humifusa – Alpine Teaberry.
Gentiana glauca – Inky Gentian.
> *G. propingua* – Fellwort.
Gentianella amarella – Northern Gentian.
> *G. tenella* – Slender Gentian.
Goodyera oblongifolia – Rattlesnake Plantain.
Heracleum lanatum – Cow Parsnip.
Hieracium albiflorum – White Hawkweed.
> *H. gracile* – Alpine Hawkweed.
Hippurus vulgaris.
Huechera micrantha.
Huperzia selago – Ground Fir.
Hypopitys monotropa – Pinesap.
Juniper communis – Common Juniper.
Kalmia polifolia – Bog-laurel.

Ledum palustris spp. *groenlandicum* – Labrador Tea.
Leptarrhena pyrolifolia – Leather-leaved Saxifrage.
Lestera cordata.
Leutkea pectinata – Partridge Foot.
Lewisia pygmeia – Pigmy Lewisia.
Linnaea borealis – Twinflower.
Lithophragma parviflora – Fringe Cup.
Lloydia serotina – Alp Lily.
Loiseleuria procumbens – Creeping Azalea.
Lonicera involucrata – Bracted Honeysuckle.
Lupinus arcticus – Arctic Lupin.
    L. lyalli – Lyall's Lupin.
Lycopodium alpinum – Alpine Club Moss.
    L. annotinum – Running Club Moss.
    L. inundata.
Menyanthes trifoliata – Bog Bean, Buckbean.
Mimulus breweri – Brewer's Monkeyflower.
    M. guttatus – Common Monkeyflower.
    M. lewisii – Pink Monkeyflower.
    M. tinlingiii – Alpine Monkeyflower.
Minuarta austromontana – Mountain Pearlwort.
    M. obtusiloba.
    M. rubella.
Mitella nuda – Mitrewort.
    M. pentandra.
    M. trifida.
Monesis uniflora – Single Delight.
Myosotis alpina – Alpine Forgetmenot.
Nuphar polysepalum – Yellow Pond-lily.
Osmorhiza chilensis – Sweet Cicily.
    O. purpurea (one plant) – Purple Sweet Cicily.
Oxyria digyna – Mountain Dock.
Parnassia fimbriata – Fringed Grass of Parnassus.
    P. palustris – Marsh Grass of Parnassus.
Paxistima myrsinites – False Box.
Pedicularis lyalli – Lyall's Lousewort.
    P. ornithorhyncha – Bird's Beak Lousewort.
    P. parviflora – Small-flowered Lousewort.
    P. recemosa – Racemose Lousewort.
Penstemmon davidsonii.
    P. procerus – Small Blue Penstemon.
    P. serratus – Western Penstemon.
Petasites nivalis (frigidus) – Alpine Coltsfoot.
    P. palmatus – Coltsfoot.
Phacelia sericea var. *sericea* – Silky Phacelia.
Phyllodoce empetriformis – Pink Mountain Heather.
    P. glandulifera – Yellow Mountain Heather.
    P. intermedia.
*Picea glauca X englemannii – Spruce sp.
Pinguicula vulgaris – Common Butterwort.
Pinus albicaulis – Whitebark Pine.
    P. contorta – Lodgepole Pine.

Plantantheria dilatata – White Bog-orchid.
        P. hyperborea – Green Bog-orchid.
        P. obtusa – Blunt-leaved Orchid.
        P. unalaskensis – Alaskan Rein Orchid.
Polemonium pulcherrimum – Jacob's Ladder.
Polygonum mimimum Small Knotweed.
        P. viviparum – Alpine Knotweed.
Populus balsamifera (occasional shrubs at treeline) – Cottonwood.
        P. tremuloides – Trembling Aspen.
Potamogeton alpinus – Alpine Pondweed.
Potentilla arguta.
        P. diversifolia – Diverse-leaved Cinquefoil.
        *P. flabelliforlia.
        P. palustris – Marsh Cinqefoil.
        P. villosa – Hairy Cinqefoil.
Pyrola asarifolia – Large-leaved Wintergreen.
        P. chlorantha – Green Wintergreen.
        P. minor.
        P. sucunda var. *secunda* – One-sided Wintergreen.
Ranunculus aquatilis var. *capillaceus* – Water Crowfoot.
        R. exchcholtzii – Alpine Meadow Buttercup.
        R. flammulata ssp *reptans* – Creeping Spearwort.
        *R. gelidus.
        R. pygmaeus – Pigmy Buttercup.
Rhododendron albiflorum – White Mountain Rhododendron.
Ribes lacustre – Swamp Currant.
        R. laxiflorum – Trailing Currant.
        R. viscossisimum – Sticky Currant.
Romanzoffia sitchensis – Mist Maiden.
Rubus idaeus – Raspberry.
        R. parviflorus – Thimbleberry.
        R. pedatus – Creeping Raspberry.
Rumex acetosa – Sheep Sorrel.
*Sagina crassicaulis.
Salix arctica – Arctic Willow.
        S. brachycarpa.
        S. commutata.
        S. lucida.
        S. nivalis – Snow Willow.
        S. pedicellaris.
        S. sitchenisis.
Sanguisorba sitchensis – Sitka Burnet.
Saxifraga adcendens – Wedge-leaved Saxifrage.
        S. bronchialis var. *austromontana* – Spotted Saxifrage.
        S. caespitosa – Creeping Saxifrage.
        S. cernua – Nodding Saxifrage.
        S. debilis.
        S. ferruginea – Rusty Saxifrage.
        S. lyalli – Red-stemmed Saxifrage.
        S. mertensiana – Woodland Saxifrage.
        S. occidentalis – Western Saxifrage.
        S. oppositifolia – Purple Saxifrage.

S. punctata – Dotted Saxifrage.

S. tolmiei – Tolmei's Saxifrage.

Sedum divergens – Berry-leaved Stonecrop.

S. lanceolatum – Lance-leaved Stonecrop.

S. roseum – Roseroot.

Selaginella densa.

Senecio canus – Mountain Butterweed.

S. parviflorus – Small-flowered Groundsel.

S. triangularis – Spear-leafed Groundsel.

Shepherdia canadensis – Soap Berry.

Sibbaldia procumbens.

Silene acaulis – Moss Campion.

S. parryi.

Solidago multiradiata – Mountain Goldenrod.

Sorbus sitchensis var. *sitchensis* – Sitka Mountain Ash.

Spiraea pyramidata – Pyramid Spiraea.

Spiranthes romanzoffiana – Ladies Tresses.

Sporganium angustifolium.

S. hyperboreum.

Stelleria longipes – Mountain Meadow Starwort.

S. nitens – Shining Starwort.

S. umbellata – Creeping Starwort.

Streptopus amplexifolius – Clasping-leaved Twisted Stalk.

S. roseus – Rosy Twisted Stalk.

Subularia aquatica.

Suksdorfia ranunculifolia – Buttercup-leaved Suksdorfia.

Taraxum ceratophorum – Horned Dandelion.

T. officinale – Common Dandelion.

Thuja plicata (dwarfed) – Western Red Cedar.

Tiarella trifolium var. *uniflora* – Mountain Foam Flower.

Tofielda glutinosa var. *brevistyla* – Sticky Onion.

Trientalis arctica – Northern Star Flower.

Trollius laxus var. *albiflora* – Globe Flower.

Tsuga heterophylla (dwarfed) – Mountain Hemlock.

T. mertensiana (Possible hybrids) – Western Hemlock.

Vaccinium caespitosum – Creeping Blueberry.

V. membranaceum – Black Huckleberry.

V. oxycoccus – Dwarf Cranberry.

V. uliginosum – Bog Blueberry.

Valeriana sitchensis – Sitka Valerian.

Veratrum viride – False Hellebore.

Veronica alpina – Alpine Speedwell.

Vibernum edule – Highbush Cranberry.

Viola adunca – Early Purple Violet.

V. orbiculata – Round-leaved Violet.

V. palustris – Marsh Violet.

*Woodsia scopulina.

Many sedges, rushes and grasses not catalogued.

NUK TESSLI BIRDS

sp = Spring, s = Summer, f = Fall,
w = Winter, occ. = Occasional
n = Nests

Blackbird
    Brewers – sp, s occ.
    Redwing – sp very rarely.
Bluebird, Mountain – s occ.
Chickadee, Mountain – year round, n.
Cowbird, Brown-headed – s occ.
Crow – s, w, occ.
Dipper, American – w at cabin elevation,
    s in alpine, n.
Eagle, Bald – yr round
Finch
    Grey crowned rosy (grey headed race)
      – s alpine, .n
    Purple – w, occ.
Flicker, Red-shafted – sp, s.
Flycatcher, Olive-sided – sp, s, f, n.
Golden-eye, Barrow's – s, n.
Goose
    Brant – f, occ.
    Canada – s, f, not many.
Mallard – s.
Grebe
    Horned – f.
    Redneck – f.
    Western – f.
Grosbeak, Pine – all year but not
    common.
Grouse Blue – sp, s, f, n.
Grouse Spruce – sp, s, f, n.
Heron, Great blue – s, f, occ.
Hummingbird, Rufous – sp, s, one young
    once.
Jaeger, Long-tailed – s, occ.
Jay
    Grey – all year.
    Stellar's – sp, s, f, occ.
Junco
    Dark-eyed – sp, s, f, n
    Snow bunting – sp, occ.
Kestrel, American – s, occ.
Killdeer – s, occ.
Kingfisher, Belted – late s.
Kinglet, Ruby-crowned – sp, s, f, n.
    Gold-crowned – sp, f.
Lark, Horned – s (alpine only), n.

Loon
    Common – sp, s, f, usually 2 pr per year
      on lake, n, occ.
    Pacific – f, occ.
Merganzer, Common – sp, s, f, n.
Merlin – sp, s, f, occ.
Nutcracker, Clark's – all year, n.
Nuthatch, Red-breasted – year round, n.
Osprey – s, f, occ.
Owl
    Great Horned – all year, occ.
    Hawk – s, once.
    Sawwhet – occ.
Pine siskin – s, f, occ.
Ptarmigan
    Rock – s, n.
    White-tailed – s, n.
    Willow – s in alpine, w in forest, n.
Raven – all year, not common except f.
Red poll – late w, occ.
Robin – sp, s, f, commoner in alpine, n.
Sandpiper
    Semipalmated – s.
    Solitary – s, uncommon.
    Spotted – sp, s, f, n.
Sapsucker, Yellow-bellied – s, occ.
Scoter
    Surf – sp, f.
    White-winged – f.
Shoveller – f, occ.
Shrike, Northern – late w, occ.
Sparrow,
    Fox – sp, s, f, n.
    Gold-crowned – sp cabin level, s
      alpine, n.
    Savannah – s, f, n.
    White-crowned – sp cabin level, s
      alpine.
Swallow
    Barn – s, occ, n, occ. Not seen for a
      decade.
    Tree – sp, s, n.
Swan, Trumpeter – w, uncommon.
Swift, Black – s.
Teal, Greenwinged – sp, occ.
Thrush,
    Hermit – sp, s, n.
    Varied – sp, s, f.
Warbler
    Black-polled – s, n.
    Wilson's – s.
    Yellow-rumped – sp, s, f, n.

Starling – sp occ, s occ.
Water pipit – s (alpine).
Waxwing
    Bohemian – f, occ.
    Cedar – f.
Western Wood Peewee – occ.
Woodpecker, Downy – w, f.
    Hairy – year-round, n.
    Three-toed – sp, s, n.
Wren, Winter – sp, s, f, n.

Index of Species in *A Mountain Year*

caddisfly (*Brachycentrus americanus*) **121**, 122
Calidris pusilla (sandpiper) 71, 128
Caltha leptosepala (mountain marsh marigold) **58**, 64, 77, 93, **94–95**, 146
Campanula lasiocarpa (alpine harebell) 139
Campanula rotundifolia (round-leaved/common harebell) **139**
Canis lupus (wolf) 4
caribou, mountain (*Rangifer tarandus caribou*) **124**, 125, 147
Cassiope mertensiana (white mountain-heather) **82**, 83, 84, 96, 120
Castilleja miniata (common red paintbrush) 96, **107**, 108, 116–**117**,120, 124
Castilleja parviflora (small-flowered paintbrush) 96, 116–**117**, 120, 124
Catharus guttatus (hermit thrush) **64**, 73, 83, 87, 90, 108, 121, 137
cedar, western red (*Thuja plicata*) **vii**, 86
Ceratopogonidae sp (no-see-ums) 132
Ceryle alcyon (kingfisher belted) 129, 130, 138
chickadee
    black-capped (*Poecile atricapillus*) *38*
    chestnut-backed (*Poecile rufescens*) 38
    mountain (*Poecile gambeli*) **12**, 13, 14, **15**, 27, 30, 32, 33, 37, 38, 40, 41, 46, 73, 87
chipmunk, yellow pine (*Eutamias amoenus*) **46**
Chlosyne palla (northern checkerspot) **42**, 130
Cinclus mexicanus (American dipper) **18**, 32, 33, 37, **148**, 149, 156
cinquefoil
    varied-leaved/or diverse-leaved (*Potentilla diversifolia*) 116
    villous (*Potentilla villosa*) 79, **83**, 96
Clangula hyemalis (long-tailed duck/formerly oldsquaw) **155**, 156
Colaptes auratus (northern/red-shafted flicker) 34, **35**, 52, 54, 75, 80, 105–**106**, 108–109, 139
columbine, western (*Aquilegia formosa*) **114**
Contopus cooperi (olive-sided flycatcher) **75**, 81, 108
Cornus canadensis (bunchberry/creeping dogwood) 96, 129
Corvus brachyrhynchos (common crow) 64, 156
Corvus corax (common raven) 64, 138, **154**, 156
cottonwood (*Populus balsamifera*) **vii**, 86
cranberry
    bog (*Vaccinium oxycoccus*) 7–8
    highbush (*Viburnum edule*) 7, 151
Crepis elegans (elegant hawk's-beard) 126
crow, common (*Corvus brachyrhynchos*) 64, 156
crowberry (*Empetrum nigrum*) **62**
Culex pipiens (mosquito) **46**, 57, 78, 79, 85, 99, 132, 134
Cyanositta stelleri (Steller's jay) **23**, 26, 30, 34, 140–**141**
Cygnus buccinator (trumpeter swan) **156**–**157**
Cypseloides niger (black swift) **91**, 92, 149

dandelion, common (*Taraxacum officinale*) **92**–93, 96, 108,
deermouse (*Peromyscus maniculatus*) **11**, 22, 34
Dendragapus obscurus (blue grouse) 53, 80, **112**
Dendroctonus ponderosae (mountain pine beetle) **48**–49, 78, 138
Dendroica coronata (yellow-rumped warbler) 46, **47**, 57, 58, **59**, 64, 73, 108, 112, 140, 146
Dendroica striata (blackpoll warbler) **79**, 81, 90, 108, 121
dipper, American (*Cinclus mexicanus*) **18**, 32, 33, 37, **148**, 149, 156
draba
    ashy (*Draba cinerea*) 96
    lance-fruited (*Draba oligosperma*) 46, 79, **82**, 83, 96
    Payson's (*Draba paysonii*) 46, 79, **82**, 83, 96
Draba cinerea (ashy draba) 96
Draba oligosperma (lance-fruited draba) 46, 79, **82**, 83, 96
Draba paysonii (Payson's draba) 46, 79, **82**, 83, 96
dragonfly (*Anisoptera* spp) 130, **132**
Drosera longifolia (long-leaved sundew) 100
Drosera rotundifolia (round-leaved sundew) 100
Dryas octapetala (eight-petal avens/or white mountain-avens) 96, **97**

eagle, bald (*Haliaeetus leucocephalus*) **50**–51, 59–60, 73, 79, 87, 91, 102, 129, 135
Empetrum nigrum (crowberry) **62**
Epilobium anagallidifolium (alpine willowherb) 126
Epilobium latifolium (mountain fireweed/or broad-leaved willowherb) **125**–126,146, **147**
Equisetum fluviatile (water horsetail) 151–152
Erebia rossii (Ross' alpine butterfly) 130, **131**
Eremophila alpestris (horned lark) 84
Erigeron compositus (cut-leaved fleabane/or cut-leaved daisy) **126**
Erigeron peregrinus (alpine fleabane/or subalpine daisy) 126, 147
Eutamias amoenus (yellow pine chipmunk) **46**

Falcipennis canadensis (spruce grouse) 12, 41, 53, 80, 138
fir, subalpine (*Abies lasiocarpa*) **vii**, **8**, 98, 139, **161**
fireweed, mountain/or broad-leaved willowherb (*Epilobium latifolium*) **125**–126, 146, **147**

swift, black (*Cypseloides niger*) **91**, 92, 149
Synaptomys borealis (northern bog lemming) 12, 71

Tabanidae family (common horsefly) 132–**133**, 134
Tachycineta bicolor (tree swallow) **41**, 42, 52, 92, 109, **112**, 113
Tamiasciurus hudsonicus (red squirrel) **3**, 23, 24, 34
Taraxacum officinale (common dandelion) **92**–93, 96, 108
teal, green-winged (*Anas crecca*) **51**–**52**, 54
thrush
    hermit (*Catharus guttatus*) **64**, 73, 83, 87, 90, 108, 121, 137
    varied (*Ixoreus naevius*) **40**, 41, 64, 70, 83, 156
Thuja plicata (western red cedar) **vii**, 86
toad, western (*Bufo boreas*) **84**–85
Tringa solitaria (solitary sandpiper) 71
Troglodytes troglodytes (winter wren) **37**, 96, 97, 138
Trollius Laxus var. *albiflora* (globe flower) **58**, 77, 87, 93
trout, rainbow (*Oncorhynchus mykiss*) 97
Tsuga heterophylla (western hemlock) vii
Tsuga mertensiana (mountain hemlock) vii
Turdus migratorius (american robin) 38, **39**, 40, 41, 43, 46, 50, 58, 73, 83, 87, 98, 120, 137, 140, 156

Ursus americanus (black bear) 77, 141
Ursus arctos (grizzly bear) 77, 126, 143–144
Utricularia vulgaris (common bladderwort) 100

Vaccinium membranaceum (black huckleberry) 68, 79, 90, **136**, 151
Vaccinium oxycoccus (bog cranberry) 7–8
Vanessa cardui (painted lady butterfly) 130, **131**
Vespidae sp (yellowjacket/wasp) 90
Vibernum edule (highbush cranberry) 7, 151
Viola orbiculata (round-leaved violet) 72, 79
Viola palustris (marsh violet) 86, 87, 99, 102
violet
    marsh (*Viola palustris*) **86**, 87, 99, 102
    round-leaved (*Viola orbiculata*) 72, 79
vole, red-backed (*Myodes rutilus*) 12, **22**, 71
Vulpes vulpes (red fox) 20, 26, 37, 161

warbler
    blackpoll (*Dendroica striata*) **79**, 81, 90, 108, 121
    yellow-rumped (*Dendroica coronata*) 46, **47**, 57, 58, **59**, 64, 73, 108, 112, 140, 146
water horsetail (*Equisetum fluviatile*) 151–152
water strider (*Gerris remigis*) 69, **70**
waxwing, bohemian (*Bombycilla garrulous*) 138

weasel, common (*Mustela erminea*) 26, 34, 161
willow (*Salix*) var. 4, 26, **55**–56
    arctic (*Salix arctica*) 147
    pacific (*Salix lucida*) 26, **143**
    snow (*Salix reticulata* var. *nivalis*) 26, 140
    variable (*Salix commutate*) 26, 90, 143
willowherb, alpine (*Epilobium anagallidifolium*) 126
wolf (*Canis lupus*) 4
    tracks 22, 26, 30, 54, 74
woodpecker
    downy (*Picoides pubescens*) 10
    hairy (*Picoides villosus*) 9, **10**, 12, 15, 23, 28, 59, 80, 87, 106, 109
    three-toed (*Picoides tridactylu*) **81**, 102, 106
wren, winter (*Troglodytes troglodytes*) **37**, 96, 97, 138

yellowjacket/wasp (*Vespidae* sp) 90

Zonotrichia atricapilla (golden-crowned sparrow) **44**, 45, 77, 82, 98, 128

Published by
Harbour Publishing Co. Ltd.
P.O. Box 219, Madeira Park, BC, V0N 2H0
www.harbourpublishing.com

Edited by Mary Schendlinger
Text design by Roger Handling
Printed in China

Harbour Publishing acknowledges financial support from the Government of
Canada through the Book Publishing Industry Development Program and the
Canada Council for the Arts, and from the Province of British Columbia through
the BC Arts Council and the Book Publishing Tax Credit.

THE CANADA COUNCIL | LE CONSEIL DES ARTS
FOR THE ARTS | DU CANADA
SINCE 1957 | DEPUIS 1957

BRITISH
COLUMBIA
ARTS COUNCIL
Supported by the Province of British Columbia

Library and Archives Canada Cataloguing in Publication

Czajkowski, Chris
    A mountain year : nature diary of a wilderness dweller /Chris Czajkowski.
Includes index.
ISBN 978-1-55017-441-0
1. Czajkowski, Chris—Diaries. 2. Artists—Canada—Diaries. 3. Frontier and
pioneer life—British Columbia. 4. Natural history—Coast Mountains (B.C.).
5. Natural history—Coast Mountains (B.C. and Alaska)—Pictorial works. I. Title.
FC3845.C56C832008   971.1'1   C2008-904254-9

*Chris Czajkowski can be contacted by writing to the Nuk Tessli Alpine Experience,
Nimpo Lake, British Columbia, V0L 1R0, Canada, or through* www.nuktessli.ca

Map of Nuk Tessli
Immediate Surroundings

N

1 km.

Beach Ck

Big Be

Red Bea

Cohen Lk.

Portage

To Boundary Lk

Old trap Cabin

to Genhau Valley